W9-BPL-880

• T R O P H I E S •

Practice Book

Grade 2 • Volume One

Harcourt

Orlando   Boston   Dallas   Chicago   San Diego

Visit *The Learning Site!*
www.harcourtschool.com

Printed in the United States of America

ISBN 0-15-323510-1

7 8 9 10 054 10 09 08 07 06 05 04

Contents

JUST FOR YOU

Name _____

▶ **Finish the story. On each line, write a word
from the box.**

hid	slide	ride	wide
did	inside	slid	hide

A Day at the Zoo

Today we took a **(1)** __ride__ to the zoo. We saw a

chameleon. It **(2)** __slide__ in the leaves. We saw a bear.

It **(3)** __hid__ down a **(4)** _____. We saw a

lion. It opened its mouth **(5)** __inside__ and roared.

The hippo tried to **(6)** __hide__. It stayed

(7) __inside__ its house. We **(8)** __did__ enjoy

our visit!

SCHOOL-HOME CONNECTION Invite your child to
draw pictures of animals riding, sliding, and hiding.
Help him or her write sentences to go with them.

1

Practice Book
Just for You

© Harcourt

Name _____

▶ Read the Spelling Words. Sort the words
and write them where they belong.

Spelling Words

Words with *id*	Words with *ide*
1. _____	5. _____
2. _____	6. _____
3. _____	7. _____
4. _____	8. _____
	9. _____
	10. _____

hide
slide
ride
wide
pride
bid
kid
eyelid
inside
hid
no
big
brown
eat
people

▶ Write the words that are left in alphabetical
order.

11. _____	14. _____
12. _____	15. _____
13. _____	

© Harcourt

Name _____

▶ **Circle and write the word that completes each sentence.**

1. A chameleon _____*hid*_____ in the leaves.

   (hid)   hike   hip

2. The chameleon wanted to _____*ride*_____ on a bird's back.

   rope   right   (ride)

3. The chameleon did not want to _____*slide*_____ off.

   (sled)   (slide)   sleep

4. The chameleon was full of _____*pride*_____.

   pad   (pride)   peddle

5. A bird spread its wings _____*wide*_____.

   warm   (wide)   will

6. The chameleon _____*sled*_____ down a stem.

   slip   said   slid

7. He tried to _____ in the bird's wings.

   high   hide   had

8. A _____*kid*_____ saw the chameleon.

   (kid)   kind   kilt

© Harcourt

SCHOOL-HOME CONNECTION Encourage your child to write a story about what it would be like to be a chameleon. Have your child use words with -ide and -id. Ask him or her to point out those words.

3

Practice Book
Just for You

Name _____

▶ **On the lines, write the words from the box that match the clues.**

dull	exciting	handsome	hardly
sideways	sparkling	spotted	

1. You can ___hardly___ see the tiny bird on this big animal!

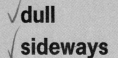

2. ___handsome___ very good-looking

3. ___dull___ tells about a color that doesn't shine

4. ___exciting___ lots of fun to watch

5. ___Side ways___ to the left or to the right

6. Have you ___spotted___ the shy crab?

7. It's sunny and the water is ___Sparkiling___.

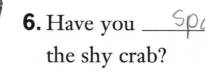

 TRY THIS! Write a letter to a friend about a trip to the zoo. In your letter, use as many Vocabulary Words as you can.

© Harcourt

Practice Book
Just for You

Name _____

Skill Reminder   A sentence tells a complete thought. It begins with a capital letter and ends with an end mark. The words are in an order that makes sense.

▶ Read each group of words. If the group is a sentence, write *sentence* on the line. If it is not a sentence, write *no*.

1. the chameleon's sticky tongue   _____

2. The chameleon caught a fly.   _____

3. on the flower   _____

4. What color is the flower?   _____

▶ Put each group of words together in sentence order. Write the sentence on the line.

5. was hungry.   chameleon   The

_____

6. a leaf.   sat on   The animal

_____

7. you   Are   hungry?

_____

8. flies?   like   Do you

_____

Practice Book
Just for You

Name _____

▶ **Write the number of syllables you hear in each
picture name.**

coat

1. __1__

bike

2. __2__

lizard

3. __2__

lion

4. __2__

baseball

5. __2__

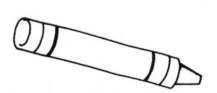

crayon

6. __2__

cowboy

7. __2__

bubbles

8. __2__

gum

9. __1__

© Harcourt

Practice Book
Just for You

Name _____

▶ **Read the paragraph. Then choose the best answer to each question. Fill in the circle next to your choice.**

Friday's Trip

Ana's class will go to the zoo. The trip is planned for Friday. Ana will visit the monkey house. She also hopes to see the seals and the big cats. Ana likes teddy bears. She can't wait until Friday.

1 What is the main idea of the paragraph?

○ Ana likes to see the elephants.

○ Ana will see seals at the zoo.

◉ Ana's class will go to the zoo.

○ Ana has never been to a zoo.

💡 **Tip**

The first sentence is often the main idea.

2 Which sentence does not belong in the paragraph?

○ Ana will visit the monkey house.

◉ Ana likes teddy bears.

○ The trip is planned for Friday.

○ She can't wait until Friday.

💡 **Tip**

Look for the answers that make the least sense.

SCHOOL-HOME CONNECTION With your child, read a favorite story. Ask your child what he or she thinks is the main idea of the story.

7

Practice Book
Just for You

© Harcourt

Name _____

▶ **Look at the Table of Contents page. Then answer the questions.**

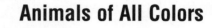

Animals of All Colors

1 What is the title of the book? ─────

⬤ Animals of All Colors

○ Table of Contents

○ Red Fox

Tip

The title of the book is the name of the book.

2 Which chapter is about ─────
yellow giraffes?

○ Chapter One

○ Chapter Two

 Chapter Three

Tip

Look at the name of each chapter. Look at the number of each chapter.

3 Which page does Chapter Four start on?

○ page 5

○ page 10

 page 15

SCHOOL-HOME CONNECTION With your child, look through a book with a table of contents. Show your child how to find the various chapters.

8

Practice Book
Just for You

Name _____

▶ **Circle the best answer to each riddle.**

1. This is another word for a baby goat. made **kid** fib

2. You go on this at an amusement park. wade toad **ride**

3. Lizards do this so no one will see them. **hide** hind help

4. This word means **not** narrow. **wide** wind will

5. This is what you do on the ice. slop **slide** skin

6. This is something a bird does in the sky. glue glare **glide**

7. This woman is getting married. broom **bride** read

8. This is something that covers a pot. lime **lid** lit

© Harcourt

SCHOOL-HOME CONNECTION Help your child make riddle cards. Fold a sheet of paper in half. Ask your child to write the riddle on the outside page. Encourage him or her to use words with -ide or -id. On the inside page, ask your child to write the riddle answer.

9

Practice Book
Just for You

Name _____

▶ **Write the words where they belong in the chart. Then write four more words of your own in each column.**

take	same	make	name
mistake	snake	game	became

<u>br**ake**</u>	<u>fl**ame**</u>
snake	game
make	became
take	name
mistake	same

SCHOOL-HOME CONNECTION Talk with your child about their morning routine. Encourage your child to use the words from this page in the discussion, for example, "I make my bed. I call the dog's name. I take the dog for a walk."

10

Practice Book
Just for You

© Harcourt

▶ **Read the Spelling Words. Sort the words and write them where they belong.**

Words with *ame*	Words with *ake*
1. name	6. brake
2. flame	7. snake
3. same	8. mistak
4. became	9. take
5. games	10. make

▶ **Sort the words that are left by the number of syllables.**

One-Syllable Words	Two-Syllable Words
11. slide	14. eye lid
12. line	**Three-Syllable words**
13. more	15. together

Spelling Words

games
take
make
name
flame
same
became
brake
snake
mistake
eyelid
slide
line
more
together

© Harcourt

Practice Book
Just for You

Name _____

▶ **Solve the riddles. Write a word from the box on each line.**

flame	take	same	make	name
brake	mistake	snake	games	became

1. People play them. They are ___games___.

2. Someone gives you something. You ___brake___ it.

3. This stops the wheels of a car or bike.

   It is a _____.

4. Something changed into something else.

   It _____ something else.

5. This is something people do wrong.

   It is a _____.

6. This is the hot part of a fire. It is the _____.

7. This is something that is exactly like something else.

   It is the _____.

8. This is what you do when you cook.

   You _____ something.

9. This is what people call you. It is your _____.

10. This animal is long and thin. It is a _____.

SCHOOL-HOME CONNECTION Exchange other riddles with your child, using the phonics words. Then pose simple riddles for your child to answer using other words.

12

© Harcourt

Practice Book
Just for You

▶ **Finish the story. On each line, write a word from the box.**

always	homework	minutes	snuggle	treat

My new puppy, Barky, **(1)** _____ barks.

He even barks while I do my **(2)** _____

for school. He barks when he is hungry and wants a

(3) _____. He also barks when he wants to

(4) _____ with me in bed when it is cold outside.

I spend ten **(5)** _____ every day trying to teach
him to be quiet.

 TRY THIS! Write a paragraph about a pet. Use as many Vocabulary Words as you can.

Practice Book
Just for You

Name _____

Skill Reminder • **A statement is a sentence that tells something. It ends with a period (.).**

• **A question is a sentence that asks something. It ends with a question mark (?).**

▶ On the line, write each group of words as a complete sentence. Begin with a capital letter. If the sentence is a statement, add a period at the end. If it is a question, add a question mark at the end.

1. is it time to go _____

2. we will go in ten minutes

_____

3. do I have to wait _____

4. why don't you want to wait _____

5. i want to go home to play with my puppy.

_____

6. what is the name of your puppy

_____

7. i call her Yup _____

8. that is a funny name. _____

Write three questions about puppies. Then write three answers.

Practice Book
Just for You

Name _____

▶ **Find the word that has the same sound as the underlined letters in the first word.**

Example: b<u>ake</u>

    ○ name

    ○ bike

    ○ lake

1 t<u>ame</u>

    ○ take

    ◉ lame

    ○ tap

> **Tip**
> Listen for the sound made by the underlined letters.

2 cornfl<u>ake</u>

    ◉ shake

    ○ game

    ○ came

3 sh<u>ame</u>

    ○ shake

    ○ ram

    ◉ flame

> **Tip**
> Read each answer choice carefully before you decide.

© Harcourt

Practice Book
Just for You

Name _____

▶ **Read the signs. Then answer each question.**
Write your answer on the line.

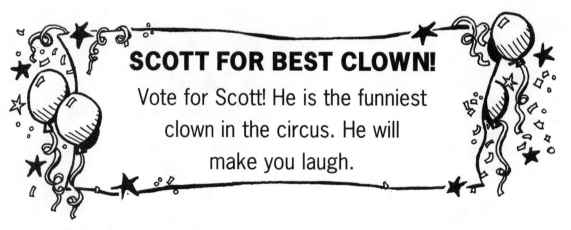

BE ON TIME FOR SCHOOL!
You have to be in school by 8:30 in the morning.
That is when all classes start. Here is what you can do to be
on time. Lay out your clothes the night before. Pack your
backpack the night before. Wake up early. Be sure to eat a
good breakfast. Get to the bus stop ten minutes
before the bus comes.

What was the author's purpose for writing this sign?

_____

_____

SCOTT FOR BEST CLOWN!
Vote for Scott! He is the funniest
clown in the circus. He will
make you laugh.

What was the author's purpose for writing this sign?

_____

_____

SCHOOL-HOME CONNECTION Look at a few
types of writing with your child, such as recipes,
instructions, and advertisements. Ask your child
why the author wrote each type.

16

Practice Book
Just for You

© Harcourt

Name _____

▶ **Write the words from the box that best
complete the poem. Remember that the word
you write should rhyme with the last word in the line above.**

inside	eyelid	kid	slide

The strange chameleon would not hide.

In the grass it liked to _____.

One day it saw a nice, shy kid.

It winked and blinked just one _____.

The kid began to swell with pride.

He took the lizard back _____.

But the lizard went and hid.

Then it said, "Well, so long, _____."

SCHOOL-HOME CONNECTION Ask your child
to draw pictures of a lizard hiding. Help your child
write sentences to go with the picture. For
example, "A lizard could hide under the leaves."

17

Practice Book
Just for You

Name _____

▶ **Complete the picture labels. Write a word from the box on each line.**

mailed	barked	finished	licked
painted	checked	thanked	opened

1. The dog _____ loudly.

The cat _____ its paw.

2. Esther _____ the

mailbox and _____
the letter.

3. José _____ the test

and _____
his answers.

4. Carl _____ the woman

who _____
his house.

SCHOOL-HOME CONNECTION Act out one of the action words. Challenge your child to guess your action and supply the correct word. Encourage your child to act out an action for you to guess.

18

Practice Book
Just for You

© Harcourt

Name _____

▶ **Read the Spelling Words. Write each word where it belongs.**

Words with *ed*	
1. _____	6. _____
2. _____	7. _____
3. _____	8. _____
4. _____	9. _____
5. _____	10. _____

Spelling Words

barked
licked
backed
thanked
painted
opened
mailed
remarked
checked
finished
mistake
became
about
few
same

▶ **Sort the words that are left by the number of syllables.**

One-Syllable Words	Two-Syllable Words
11. _____	13. _____
12. _____	14. _____
	15. _____

© Harcourt

19

► **Circle and write the word that best completes
each sentence.**

1. "What a great day!"

   I _____.   **floated   thanked   remarked**

2. I _____
   the door.   **laughed   opened   mailed**

3. First, I _____
   a letter.   **mailed   called   pulled**

4. Then I _____
   my dog's house.   **helped   painted   counted**

5. I _____ it
   by lunchtime.   **pushed   brushed   finished**

6. I _____
   up a few steps.   **stacked   backed   packed**

7. I _____
   my paint job.   **picked   checked   folded**

8. Then my dog
   _____ happily.   **barked   stopped   pulled**

9. My dog _____
   my face.   **leaped   barked   licked**

10. My dog _____
    me.   **remarked   thanked   opened**

SCHOOL-HOME CONNECTION Encourage your
child to make up another short story that uses the
phonics words. Let your child illustrate the story, too.

20

Practice Book
Just for You

© Harcourt

Name _____

▶ **Read the clues on the leaves. On the lines, write the words from the box that match the clues.**

| chipmunks | picked | sniffing | south | woods |

(1) You find many trees here.

woods

(2) If you are doing this, you may smell something.

sniffing

(3) These are little animals.

Chipmunks

(4) You did this when you pulled fruit off a tree.

picked

(5) This is where birds fly in the fall.

South

© Harcourt

 TRY THIS! Write two or three sentences about what you like to do in the fall. Use as many Vocabulary Words as you can.

Practice Book
Just for You

Name _____

Henry and Mudge
Under the Yellow
Moon

Grammar:
Commands and
Exclamations

Skill Reminder • **A command is a sentence that tells someone to do something. It ends with a period (.).**

• **An exclamation is a sentence that shows strong feeling. It ends with an exclamation point (!).**

▶ On the line, write each group of words as a complete sentence. Begin with a capital letter. If the sentence is a command, add a period at the end. If it is an exclamation, add an exclamation point at the end.

1. look at that tree, Spot _____

2. oh, that tree is so tall _____

3. please don't chew on the branch

_____

4. wow, what a big nest that is _____

5. don't scare the bird, Spot _____

6. wow, that must be an eagle's nest

_____

7. stay away from the nest, Spot

_____

8. I am so curious _____

© Harcourt

Practice Book
Just for You

Name _____

▶ **Find the word that has the same sound as the underlined letters in the first word. Fill in the circle next to your choice.**

Example: bark<u>ed</u>

○ tamed

○ waited

○ licked

1 patt<u>ed</u> ────────────

○ hitched

○ hunted

○ mailed

💡 **Tip**

Sound out each answer choice. Listen for the sound in the underlined letters.

2 nail<u>ed</u> ────────────

○ ticked

○ lined

○ petted

💡 **Tip**

Read over your answer choice to make sure you marked the answer you wanted to mark.

23

Name _____

HOMEWORK

Henry and Mudge
Under the Yellow
Moon

Narrative Elements
TEST PREP

▶ **Read the paragraph. Then choose the best answer to each question. Fill in the circle next to your choice.**

Sam's Days

Sam always has a great time with his grandma and grandpa. He stays with them every August. Each morning, he takes a long walk with their dog, Blue. On his walk, he says hello to the horses in the barn. Then he watches Grandpa feed the pigs. Sam says, "I like the pigs best."

1 Where is Sam?

○ on a farm

○ in a city

○ in a school

> 💡 **Tip**
> Part of the setting is where the story takes place.

2 When does the story take place?

○ in the winter

○ in the fall

○ in the summer

> 💡 **Tip**
> Part of the setting is the time when the story takes place.

© Harcourt

SCHOOL-HOME CONNECTION With your child, retell a fairy tale or folktale you both enjoy. Ask your child where and when the story is set. Discuss whether or not the setting changes.

24

Practice Book
Just for You

Name _____

Henry and Mudge
Under the Yellow
Moon

Review:
Phonograms
-ame, -ake

▶ **Circle the best answer to each riddle.**

1. This is the hot part
of a fire.   fame   (flame)   name   blame

2. This is what you do
when you build.   bake   cake   (make)   take

3. This is what you do to
stop a bike.   (brake)   brain   book   braid

4. This is what people
call you.   nose   nine   (nice)   name

5. This says that two
things are alike.   sing   (same)   sum   sun

6. This is something
that is done wrong. (mistake) make   take   mane

7. This is an animal
with a long, thin body.   train   brain   brake   (snake)

SCHOOL-HOME CONNECTION Choose several
phonics words and mix up the letters. Challenge your
child to unscramble them. Let your child pose word
scrambles for you, too.

Practice Book
Just for You

Name _____

▶ **Finish the story. On each line, write a word from the box.**

tried	**cried**	**hurried**	**carried**
copied	**worried**	**studied**	**replied**

Where Is Dog?

Cat was **(1)** _____. He could not find his friend
Dog. They were going to watch a ballgame. Dog had left a

note. Cat **(2)** _____ the note to Mouse. "I can't

find Dog," Cat said. "He left a note. I **(3)** _____
to, but I can't read his writing. Can you help me?"

"Let me see," **(4)** _____ Mouse. He **(5)**

_____ the note closely. He **(6)** _____ a

few words. "Well?" **(7)** _____ Cat loudly. "Where is
he?" "Dog is at the store," said Mouse.

"He **(8)** _____ so you would not miss the ballgame.
He needed more chips and dip."

SCHOOL-HOME CONNECTION Encourage your
child to share times when he or she helped a friend.
Challenge your child to include some of the phonics
words in the discussion.

26

© Harcourt

▶ Read the Spelling Words. Sort the words
and write them where they belong.

**Spelling
Words**

**Words That Have the
Vowel Sound You Hear in *Dried***

1. _____   3. _____

2. _____   4. _____

**Words That Have the
Vowel Sound You Hear in *Emptied***

5. _____   8. _____

6. _____   9. _____

7. _____   10. _____

cried
hurried
replied
fried
tried
worried
carried
copied
married
studied
remarked
finished
alone
river
think

▶ Write the words that are left in alphabetical
order.

11. _____   14. _____

12. _____   15. _____

13. _____

© Harcourt

▶ **Solve the riddles. Write a word from the box on each line.**

carried	cried	fried	hurried
married	replied	studied	

1. This is one way people prepared food. They

   _____ it.

2. This is what two people did at a wedding. They got

   _____.

3. This is what you did to get ready for a test.

   You _____.

4. You did this when you answered a

   question. You _____.

5. This is what a baby who wasn't

   happy did. He _____.

6. This is what you did to bring

   something. You _____ it.

7. This is what you did if
   you moved quickly.

   You _____.

© Harcourt

SCHOOL-HOME CONNECTION Have fun with your child, coming up with dialogue between two friends. Include phonics words. Ask your child to write the sentences in your dialogue and underline the phonics words.

28

Practice Book
Just for You

Name _____

► **Help Turtle make a list. On each line, write a word from the pencil.**

alone ✓   cheer ✓   fine ✓
meadow ✓   reason ✓   spoiled ✓

Things to Do Today

1. Make a lunch to eat in the _meadow_.

2. Ask Bird to eat with me so I won't be _alone_.

3. Tell Bird a joke to _cheer_ her up.

4. Have a _fine_ time playing in the sun.

5. If it rains, our plans will be _spoiled_.

6. Think of a good _reason_ to go back inside.

 TRY THIS! Write a joke or a funny sentence that might make Bird laugh. Use at least one Vocabulary Word.

Practice Book
Just for You

Name _____

Skill Reminder • **The naming part of a sentence tells who or what the sentence is about. Naming parts can name two people or things. The word *and* is used to join them.**

▶ **Circle the naming part of each sentence. Then think of your own naming part. Write your new sentence.**

1. I walked home. _____

2. My best friend walked with me. _____

3. His brother came, too. _____

4. A little frog followed us. _____

5. The toad hopped after the turtle.

_____

▶ **Use the word *and* to join the naming parts of the sentences in each pair. Write your new sentence.**

6. My friend walked to school. I walked to school.

_____

7. Frog rode the bus. His friend rode the bus.

_____

Practice Book
Just for You

Syllable Rule • **When a two-syllable word has an -ed ending, the word is usually divided before the ending.**

▶ Read each word. Then add an *ed* ending to the word. Write the new word.

Base word	Base word + ending
act	1. _acting_
mend	2. _mender_
blend	3. _blender_
wait	4. _waiting_
fold	5. _folding_

▶ Read each word. Divide the two-syllable words into syllables. Write the syllables.

Word List	Divided Words
mended	6. _____
folded	7. _____
blended	8. _____
hunted	9. _____
waited	10. _____

Name _____

▶ **Read the paragraph. Then choose the best answer to each question. Fill in the circle next to your choice.**

Zeke the zebra and Snappy the snail are friends. They both like being outside. Zeke is a fast runner. Snappy is slow. Zeke likes carrots, but Snappy likes apples. Zeke likes to play. Snappy hides under a rock. "Snappy is not like me, but we are still friends," says Zeke. Zeke does all the talking. Snappy is the quiet one.

1 What is the same about Zeke and Snappy?

○ Zeke is a zebra.

○ Snappy moves slowly.

○ They both talk a lot.

● They both like being outside.

💡 **Tip**
Read the paragraph to check each answer choice.

2 What is different about Zeke and Snappy?

○ Zeke and Snappy like to eat.

○ Snappy and Zeke are animals.

● Zeke is fast and Snappy is slow.

○ Snappy and Zeke are friends.

💡 **Tip**
Remember to read each choice carefully.

© Harcourt

SCHOOL-HOME CONNECTION With your child, compare and contrast some simple items in your kitchen. For example, have your child find items that are alike because they come in boxes. Then contrast the contents of the boxes.

Practice Book
Just for You

▶ **Read the story. On each line, write the word from the box that best completes the sentence.**

remarked	finished	barked	thanked
licked	opened	painted	checked

Today I **(1)** ___painted___ a dog.

I **(2)** ___opened___ the door. The dog

came in. "What a great dog!" I **(3)** ___remarked___.

He **(4)** ___barked___ loudly.

He **(5)** ___licked___ my face. Then

we began. When I **(6)** ___finished___

the picture, I **(7)** ___checked___ my

work. The dog **(8)** ___thanked___

me with another bark and a lick.

SCHOOL-HOME CONNECTION Invite your child to illustrate the story. Help your child write new sentences for the story, using the phonics words.

33

Practice Book
Just for You

© Harcourt

▶ **Write the words where they belong in the chart.**

| acrobat | ate | flat | appreciate | fat |
| gate | create | that | state | sat |

sat	gate

SCHOOL-HOME CONNECTION Encourage your
child to think of a story that uses many of the phonics
words. Write down sentences as your child says
them. Ask your child to underline the phonics words.

34

Practice Book
Just for You

© Harcourt

▶ **Read the Spelling Words. Sort the words and write them where they belong.**

Spelling Words

Words with *at*	Words with *ate*
1. _____	6. _____
2. _____	7. _____
3. _____	8. _____
4. _____	9. _____
5. _____	10. _____

sat
ate
acrobat
flat
that
fat
gate
appreciate
create
state
worried
studied
children
each
girl

▶ **Sort the words that are left by the number of syllables.**

One-Syllable Words	Two-Syllable Words
11. _____	13. _____
12. _____	14. _____
	15. _____

© Harcourt

Name _____

▶ **Solve the riddles. Write a word from the box on each line.**

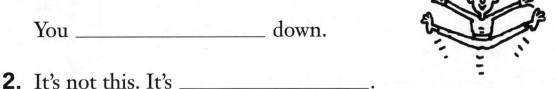

acrobat	ate	fat	flat
gate	sat	state	that

1. You didn't stand up.

You _____ down.

2. It's not this. It's _____.

3. It's not thin. It's _____.

4. This is someone who does flips.

It's an _____.

5. This is a door in a fence.

It's a _____.

6. You've already eaten. You _____.

7. This is where your city is. It's your _____.

8. This is what a pancake is. It's _____.

SCHOOL-HOME CONNECTION Say the words and ask your child to listen. For each phonogram, have your child make a funny motion. For example, wiggling for words with *-at* and dancing for words with *-ate*.

Practice Book
Just for You

Name _____

▶ **Complete the sentences below the pictures. On each line, write a word from the box. Use each word only once.**

| amazing clustered gathered raced wandered |

My friends and I

gathered

at the top of the hill.

My dog slowly

wanderd

over to watch.

We _raced_ to the finish line. More friends

_____ at the bottom of the hill to watch us.

Playing with friends is

amazing !

TRY THIS! Write a few sentences about a summer activity you enjoy. In your sentences, use as many Vocabulary Words as you can.

© Harcourt

37

Practice Book
Just for You

Skill Reminder • **The telling part of a sentence tells what someone or something is or does.**

• **Telling parts can tell about two things. The word *and* is used to join them.**

▶ **Circle the telling part of each sentence. Then think of your own telling part. Write your new sentence on the line.**

1. I go to lunch. _____

2. Andy sits alone. _____

3. I don't like to play alone. _____

4. Andy was funny today. _____

5. I am a good friend. _____

▶ **Use the word *and* to join the telling parts of the sentences in each pair. Write your new sentence on the line.**

6. The girls run. The girls play.

_____

7. The boys talk. The boys laugh.

_____

TRY THIS! Write two sentences about something you like to do. Circle the telling parts of each sentence.

Name _____

| **Syllable Rule** | • **Divide a compound word** |
| between the two smaller words in it. |
| **Example: hot / dog   sail / boat** |

▶ **Read the sentence. Find the compound word.**
Write the word in syllables.

1. The news broadcast went all over the country.

_____

2. Bookstores have lots of books for people to buy.

_____

3. Jim will pinpoint the problem by checking his addition.

_____

4. Ann did not hear what I said because she had a daydream.

_____

5. He drew a doghouse.

_____

© Harcourt

Practice Book
Just for You

Name _____

▶ **Read the paragraph. Then choose the best answer to each question. Fill in the circle next to your choice.**

Marla Reads

Marla stood at the front of the classroom. Her hands were shaking. She had never read a story to her classmates before. Her voice shook at first. Then Marla's words became louder and clearer. Everyone listened quietly. At the end, the whole class clapped. Marla took a bow and smiled. Reading aloud was fun!

1 How does Marla feel at the beginning of the story?

○ sad   ○ tired

○ nervous   ○ bored

> **Tip**
> Reread the paragraph to make sure you understand the order of events.

2 How does Marla feel at the end of the story?

○ angry   ○ sad

○ upset   ○ happy

> **Tip**
> Look for clues about how a character feels.

3 Where does Marla read the story?

○ in the classroom

○ on the playground

○ in the office

○ in the hall

> **Tip**
> Think about where Marla would most likely read to her classmates.

SCHOOL-HOME CONNECTION With your child, talk about a time when he or she tried something new. Then invite your child to write a sentence and draw a picture illustrating his or her experience.

Practice Book
Just for You

© Harcourt

Name _____

▶ **Read the story. On each line, write the word before the ending *-ed* was added.**

"I'm late!" I **(1)** <u>cried</u>. I **(2)** <u>hurried</u> out the door. I **(3)** <u>carried</u> the cake. I had to be careful. I **(4)** <u>tried</u> to walk quickly. I was **(5)** <u>worried</u> that I would be too late. I **(6)** <u>studied</u> the street signs. I was almost there! I had **(7)** <u>copied</u> the address on the cake box. Finally, I made it. "Am I on time?" I asked. Yes, the bride **(8)** <u>replied</u>. "Now we can get **(9)** <u>married</u>."

1. _____

2. _____

3. _____

4. _____

5. _____

6. _____

7. _____

8. _____

9. _____

© Harcourt

SCHOOL-HOME CONNECTION Talk with your child about funny moments when the family was running late. Encourage your child to come up with sentences that use the phonics words.

41

Name _____

▶ **Complete the sentences. On each line, write the word that has the same sound as *back*, or the same sound as *flock*.**

1. The _____ blasted off at noon.
   (rocket   ship   plane)

2. I always eat a _____ after school.
   (sandwich   apple   snack)

3. I put a _____ on my bike to keep it safe.
   (seat   lock   helmet)

4. Please _____ your bags.
   (pack   zip   close)

5. The ship left the _____ in the morning.
   (pier   dock   ramp)

SCHOOL-HOME CONNECTION Ask your child to draw him or herself on the back of a horse, with the horse pulling a wagon. In the wagon, have your child draw objects that represent each of the phonics words. Work together to label the objects with the phonics words.

Practice Book
Just for You

© Harcourt

▶ **Read the Spelling Words. Sort the words
and write them where they belong.**

Words with *ack*	Words with *ock*
1. _____	6. _____
2. _____	7. _____
3. _____	8. _____
4. _____	9. _____
5. _____	10. _____

▶ **Sort the words that are left by the number
of syllables.**

One-Syllable Words	Three-Syllable Word
11. _____	14. _____
12. _____	**Four-Syllable Word**
13. _____	15. _____

Spelling Words

black
pack
crack
snack
horseback
lock
rocket
flock
shock
clock
appreciate
acrobat
grow
last
mouse

43

© Harcourt

▶ **The picture names in each row rhyme. Write the rhyming words that have the same sound as the underlined letters.**

1.

sn<u>ack</u>

_____

2.

fl<u>ock</u>

_____

3.

s<u>ock</u>et

_____

Practice Book
Just for You

© Harcourt

Name _____

► **Help Sandy finish her letter. On each line, write a word from the box.**

enormous	granddaughter	grew
planted	strong	turnip

Dear Grandma,

Yesterday I went to see Mrs. Page and her _____,

Kate. I helped Mrs. Page and Kate pull up the vegetables they

had _____ in their garden. The plants

_____ in rows in back of their house. I pulled up a

carrot and a _____. The carrot was

_____! I had to be _____ to pull

it up by myself. Mrs. Page plans to show it at the fair!

     Love,
     Sandy

 TRY THIS! Pick two Vocabulary Words from the box above. Write one sentence using both words. Draw a picture for your sentence.

© Harcourt

Practice Book
Just for You

Name _____

Skill Reminder • **A noun names a person, a place, a thing, or an animal.**

▶ **Read the words under each line. Choose the noun. Write it on the line.**

1. The _____ pulls _____ .
   (boy   big   better)   (why   weeds   went)

2. His _____ holds the _____ .
   (some   sister   sang)   (hose   happy   hot)

3. Their _____ pick _____ .
   (friends   funny   far) (ask   apples   add)

4. A _____ runs after the _____ .
   (did   dog   does)   (by   ball   bring)

5. Two _____ sleep under the _____ .
   (cats   come   choose)   (tree   tell   tall)

6. Some _____ fly over the _____ .
   (beautiful   birds   bigger)   (go   garden   get)

7. A _____ looks for _____ .
   (may   mouse   must)   (cheese   carry   could)

 TRY THIS! Draw pictures of four things you see in your classroom. Below each picture, write the noun that names it.

Practice Book
Just for You

© Harcourt

Name _____

Skill Reminder • **When two consonants that are the same come between two vowels in a word, divide between the consonants:** *sud/den.*

▶ Read the words. Write them in syllables using a slash mark (/).

arrow   1. _____

barrel   2. _____

bottom   3. _____

comma   4. _____

dessert   5. _____

follow   6. _____

happen   7. _____

mirror   8. _____

pizza   9. _____

scissors   10. _____

traffic   11. _____

yellow   12. _____

Practice Book
Just for You

Name _____

▶ **Read the paragraph. Then choose the best answer to each question. Fill in the circle next to your choice.**

Mei's Tomatoes

Every year, Mei grows tomatoes in her back yard. She buys seeds. She puts the seeds in the soil. Then Mei waters the soil every day. The seeds grow into big red tomatoes. Mei waits until the tomatoes are ripe. Finally, Mei picks the tomatoes and gives them to her neighbors.

1 The first thing Mei does to grow tomatoes is

- ○ buy seeds.
- ○ put the seeds in soil.
- ○ water the soil.
- ○ give the tomatoes to her neighbors.

Tip
Read each question carefully. Make sure you understand it.

2 The last thing Mei does is

- ○ water the soil.
- ○ put the seeds in soil.
- ○ give the tomatoes away.
- ○ wait until they are ripe.

Tip
Look for sequence words as you read.

© Harcourt

SCHOOL-HOME CONNECTION With your child, look through a recipe for a favorite food. Talk about the sequence of the steps. Then invite your child to point out the first and last steps in the recipe.

48

Practice Book
Just for You

Name _____

▶ **Write the words from the box in alphabetical order on the lines.**

man	lawn	cat	vegetable	garden
dig	seed	turnip	soil	bird

1. bird   **6.** man

2. _____   **7.** _____

3. _____   **8.** _____

4. _____   **9.** _____

5. _____   **10.** _____

SCHOOL-HOME CONNECTION Help your child
write down the names of some classmates or friends.
Then assist your child in putting the names in
alphabetical order.

49

Practice Book
Just for You

© Harcourt

Name _____

▶ **Circle the best answer to each riddle.**

1. You did this at mealtime.

  art   ate   aim

2. An animal becomes this if it eats too much.

  fit   fine   fat

3. This is what a tire becomes if it runs over a nail.

  flat   flute   flake

4. This is what you did before you stood up.

  sale   sad   sat

5. This tells which one you mean.

  that   then   there

6. This is someone who does lots of flips.

  artist   astronaut   acrobat

7. This is something the United States has 50 of.

  stand   stamp   state

8. This is what you do when you make something.

  cart   create   crow

9. This is a door in a fence.

  garden   gift   gate

SCHOOL-HOME CONNECTION With your child,
write a funny story about an acrobat. Write
a few sentences from the story that use the phonics
words. Invite your child to illustrate the sentences.

Practice Book
Just for You

© Harcourt

Name _____

▶ **Finish the story. On each line, write a word from the box.**

pearl	earned	heard	research	learn
rehearsed	early	search	earth	

Buried Treasure

My brother woke up **(1)** _____. "Where

are you going?" I asked. "To **(2)** _____ for

buried treasure," he said. "I **(3)** _____ some
was buried out back." "I want to help!" I told him. First,

we did some **(4)** _____. We needed to

(5) _____ how to find a buried treasure.

We **(6)** _____ digging to get some practice.

Then, we dug in the **(7)** _____. But all we

found was one **(8)** _____. We felt we had

(9) _____ it.

SCHOOL-HOME CONNECTION Ask your child to
draw a picture of something else he or she could
search for. Then help your child write steps for
finding it, using the phonics words.

51

Practice Book
Just for You

© Harcourt

Name _____

▶ **Read the Spelling Words. Write each word where it belongs.**

Words with *ear*	
1. _____	6. _____
2. _____	7. _____
3. _____	8. _____
4. _____	9. _____
5. _____	10. _____
	11. _____

Spelling Words

learn
earnest
earth
heard
pearl
search
rehearse
earn
yearn
research
horseback
rocket
early
pretty
someone

▶ **Write the words that are left in alphabetical order.**

12. _____	14. _____
13. _____	15. _____

© Harcourt

52

Name ___Mal___

▶ **Circle the word that completes each sentence. Then write the word on the line.**

1. One morning, I woke up ___early___ .
   (early)   ear   eagle

2. I had to ___research___ a project for school.
   reheat   remind   (research)

3. It was about our planet, ___earth___ .
   (Earth)   easy   each

4. I ___heard___ my sister in the kitchen.
   heat   heart   (heard)

5. I ___rehearsed___ what I would say to her.
   (rehearsed)   reached   reheated

6. I ___yearned___ for her help.
   yellow   (yearned)   year

7. We ___searched___ the library that day.
   (searched)   seal   sent

8. I gave her one of my ___pearls___ .
   peel   (pearls)   pale

9. "You ___earned___ it," I told her.
   eaten   elbow   (earned)

SCHOOL-HOME CONNECTION As you and your child do tasks around the house, say sentences that use the phonics words. Challenge your child to say some to you.

53

Practice Book
Just for You

© Harcourt

▶ **Complete the sentences. On each line, write a word from the box.**

| alongside | chores | engine | simple | sprout | tool |

Hi, I'm Carmen. I work
(1) _____
Jack.

Hi, I'm Jack. I work
next to Carmen.

(2) We can help you with your _____.

(3) We do hard jobs. We do _____ jobs.

(4) If your car does not run, we can fix the _____.

(5) We can help you in your garden. We can plant and water

your seeds so they will _____. **(6)** Call us

for help! We always have the right _____ to get
the work done!

TRY THIS! Draw a picture of yourself helping someone. Then write about your picture. Use as many Vocabulary Words as you can.

© Harcourt

Skill Reminder • **Add the letter _s_ to most nouns to name more than one. Add the letters _es_ to some nouns to name more than one.**

▶ **Finish each sentence. Change the noun in ( ) to name more than one. Then write it on the line.**

1. Aunt Lucy and I do many _jobs_. **(job)**

2. I help her wash the _windows_. **(window)**

3. We wash the _dishis_, too. **(dish)**

4. Aunt Lucy and I can fix _bikes_. **(bike)**

5. Sometimes we fix _cars_, too. **(car)**

6. We have _tools_ for every job. **(tool)**

7. We keep them in _boxes_. **(box)**

TRY THIS! Write a sentence about something you like to do with your family or friends. Use a noun that names more than one. Draw a picture to go with your sentence.

| **Syllable Rule** | • **Divide a two-syllable word** |

ending in *-ing* or *-ly* between the base word and the ending.

Examples: clear / ly   chew / ing   plant / ed

                    lone / ly   turn / ing   braid / ed

• **Divide a word that ends in *-ed* before the base word if the base word ends in *t* or *d*.**

▶ Read the words in the box. Then write each word in syllables on the lines.

| burning | counted | singing | jumping | mashing |
| nearly | beaded | nicely | smoothly | waited |

1. _____   2. _____

3. _____   4. _____

5. _____   6. _____

7. _____   8. _____

9. _____   10. _____

Practice Book
Just for You

Name _____

▶ **Read the paragraph. Then choose the best answer to each question. Fill in the circle next to your choice.**

Animal Tools

Some animals use tools to help them with their daily activities. The tools can help animals find food. Sea otters use rocks to smash shells so they can eat the meat inside. Otters like to float on their backs. Other animals use parts of their bodies as tools. The beaver uses its tail to help build its home. It scoops mud onto its tail and then pats the mud between logs.

1 What is the main idea of the paragraph?

○ Sea otters smash rocks.

○ Beavers scoop mud onto their tails.

○ Some animals use tools to help them.

○ Otters like to float on their backs.

> **Tip**
> Reread the first sentence of the paragraph.

2 Which sentence does not belong in the paragraph?

○ The tools can help animals find food.

○ Otters like to float on their backs.

○ The beaver uses its tail to help build its home.

○ Other animals use parts of their bodies as tools.

> **Tip**
> Read each possible answer carefully.

SCHOOL-HOME CONNECTION Ask your child to read aloud a paragraph from a nonfiction children's book or magazine article. Then have your child tell you the main idea.

57

Practice Book
Just for You

© Harcourt

Name _____

▶ **Write words from the box to complete the poem. Remember that each word you write should rhyme with the last word in the line above.**

| rocket | snack | horseback | clock | rock | rack |

When I wake, I have a shock.

I see the hour on the _____.
I try to hurry as I pack.

Then I eat a little _____
I shut my sack and close the lock.

The pack's as heavy as a _____.
I drop the key into my pocket.

I'm out the door just like a _____.
At the barn I feed Big Jack.

His saddle waits upon the _____.
I pet my horse, so smooth and black.

Then off I go to ride _____!

SCHOOL-HOME CONNECTION Discuss with your
child a time when he or she overslept, then hurried to
be ready on time. Invite your child to draw a picture
of the event, labeling it with a sentence that uses the
phonics words.

58

Practice Book
Just for You

© Harcourt

Name _____

▶ **Write the abbreviations where they belong in the chart.**

Dec. ✓   Mr. ✓   Sun. ✓   Dr. ✓   Wed. ✓
Aug. ✓   Mrs. ✓   Jan. ✓   Tues. ✓

People	Days of the Week	Months
1. Mr.	2. Sun.	3. Dec.
4. Mrs.	5. Tues.	6. Aug.
7. Dr.	8. Wed	9. Jan.

SCHOOL-HOME CONNECTION With your child, go on a scavenger hunt through your home to find examples of these abbreviations.

59

Practice Book
Just for You

© Harcourt

▶ **Read the Spelling Words. Write the abbreviations on the lines.**

Spelling Words

Common Abbreviations	
1. _____	6. _____
2. _____	7. _____
3. _____	8. _____
4. _____	9. _____
5. _____	10. _____

Mr.
Mrs.
Dr.
Jan.
Aug.
Dec.
Tues.
Wed.
Sun.
St.
rehearse
search
before
blue
room

▶ **Write the words that are left in alphabetical order.**

11. _____	14. _____
12. _____	15. _____
13. _____	

Practice Book
Just for You

Name _____

▶ **Solve the riddles. Write an abbreviation from the box on each line.**

Tues.	Dec.	Mr.	Sun.	Jan.
Dr.	Aug.	Wed.	St.	

1. This stands for Sunday. It's _____.

2. This stands for August. It's _____.

3. This stands for Doctor.

It's _____.

4. This stands for Street.

It's _____.

5. This stands for January.

It's _____.

6. This stands for Mister. It's _____.

7. This stands for Tuesday. It's _____.

8. This stands for December. It's _____.

9. This stands for Wednesday. It's _____.

SCHOOL-HOME CONNECTION Invite your child
to write a simple letter to Mr. Putter and Tabby.
Encourage your child to use as many common
abbreviations as possible. When the letter is finished,
have your child underline each abbreviation.

61

Practice Book
Just for You

© Harcourt

Name _____

▶ **Finish the story. On each line, write a word from the box.**

cranes	directions	promise	twitch	worry

Pete got two toy _____ from his

grandparents. He needed help to put the toys together.

Pete was so sad that his nose

began to _____.

Pete called Dad. Dad made

a _____.

He said, "Don't _____.
When I get home, we will put those
toys together."

Dad and Pete read the

_____ together.

TRY THIS! What do you think happened next? Draw a picture and write a sentence.

Practice Book
Just for You

Name _____

Skill Reminder • **Some nouns change their
spelling to name more than one.**

▶ **Finish each sentence. Change the noun in ( ) to
name more than one. Then write it on the line.**

1. These _____ make toys. **(woman)**

2. Two _____ work with them. **(man)**

3. They make little _____. **(mouse)**

4. The last thing they add is _____. **(foot)**

5. They make big _____, too. **(goose)**

6. Once, they made a dog with big _____. **(tooth)**

7. Little _____ did not like that dog. **(child)**

TRY THIS! Draw a picture that shows more than one mouse and more
than one child. Write a sentence to go with your picture.
Change the nouns *mouse* and *child* to name more than one.

Practice Book
Just for You

© Harcourt

Mr. Putter and
Tabby Fly
the Plane

Common
Abbreviations
TEST PREP

▶ **Choose the correct abbreviation for each word.**
Fill in the circle next to your choice.

Example: Mister

○ Mr

○ Mr.

○ mr

1 Road

○ Rd.

○ rd

○ Rd

> **Tip**
> Most abbreviations start with a capital letter and end with a period.

2 Wednesday

○ Wd

○ wed.

○ Wed.

3 inch

○ in

○ in.

○ In.

> **Tip**
> An abbreviation for a measurement doesn't have to start with a capital letter.

© Harcourt

Name _____

▶ **Read the story beginning. Think about what will happen next. Then write the correct answer on the line.**

Mrs. Tiny always wanted to fly in a balloon. "I want to see my house from the sky," she said. One day a circus came to town. There were clowns and elephants. There was also a balloon ride.

The next day, Mrs. Tiny got up very early. She put on her flying clothes. She tucked her hair into a flying cap. "Now, I'm ready," she told herself.

1 What is Mrs. Tiny most likely to do next?

> **Tip**
> Reread the last few sentences for clues.

_____

_____

_____

2 Will Mrs. Tiny fly in a balloon?

> **Tip**
> Look for clues about planning to fly in a balloon.

_____

3 Which clue tells you what might happen?

_____

_____

_____

SCHOOL-HOME CONNECTION Read to your child the first part of a story he or she has never read. Invite your child to help you predict how it might end. Talk with your child about clues in the story that helped him or her predict.

Practice Book
Just for You

© Harcourt

Name _____

Mr. Putter and
Tabby Fly
the Plane

Review:
R-controlled
Vowels: /ûr/ ear

▶ **Read the story. On each line, write the word
that best completes each sentence.**

heard	early	earned	pearl
earth	searched	learned	

Today, we woke up **(1)** _____.
We were going to clean up the

(2) _____. We

(3) _____ an ad on

the radio. We **(4)** _____
about the cleanup day at the park.

At the park, we **(5)** _____
for trash. Someone found a pretty

(6) _____. We cleaned
the whole park. We felt we had

(7) _____ a rest.

© Harcourt

SCHOOL-HOME CONNECTION Ask your child to
write a radio ad for cleaning up a park. Encourage
your child to use the phonics words. Let your child
read or tape-record the radio ad.

66

Practice Book
Just for You

Name _____

► **Complete the story. On each line, write a word from the box.**

fourth	course	resource
four	your	poured

Ann's Course in Baking

Ann took a **(1)** _____ in baking. First she

measured **(2)** _____ cups of flour. Then she added

two eggs. Third, she added oil. **(3)** _____, she

mixed everything together. Then she **(4)** _____ it
into a cake pan.

Ann's mother gave her the recipe for the cake.

(5) "_____ cake is great," Mother told Ann.

"You can also use cookbooks as a **(6)** _____ for
cake baking, too."

© Harcourt

SCHOOL-HOME CONNECTION Ask your child
to write or tell a favorite recipe using some of the
words from this lesson.

67

Practice Book
Just for You

▶ **Read the Spelling Words. Write each word
where it belongs.**

Words with *our*	
1. _____	6. _____
2. _____	7. _____
3. _____	8. _____
4. _____	9. _____
5. _____	10. _____

**Spelling
Words**

four
poured
your
course
court
fourteen
mourn
source
fourth
resource
Dr.
St.
smell
thank
open

▶ **Sort the words that are left.**

Abbreviations	One-Syllable Words
11. _____	13. _____
12. _____	14. _____
	Two-Syllable Word
	15. _____

© Harcourt

Name _____

▶ **Solve the riddles. Write a word from the box on each line.**

fourth	course	four	fourteen
yours	resource	court	pour

1. People play tennis on it. It's a _____.

2. It's the grade after third. It's _____.

3. Race car drivers drive on this. It's a _____.

4. It's the number after three. It's _____.

5. This is not mine. It's _____.

6. When you fill a cup with a liquid, you do this.

   You _____.

7. This is the number after thirteen. It's _____.

8. A dictionary or an encyclopedia is this kind of book.

   It's a _____.

SCHOOL-HOME CONNECTION Help your child
find the different meanings of the words *course* and
court. Ask them to use each meaning in a sentence.

69

Practice Book
Just for You

© Harcourt

Name _____

▶ **Finish the directions that June's mom left for
her and her dad. On each line, write a word from the box.**

batter	buttery	perfect
recipe	smeared	yellow cake

1. First, read the _____.

2. Then, mix the _____.

3. Make sure you have

_____ butter on the

inside of the pan.

4. The sides must be _____, too.

Pour the batter into the pan. Put the pan in the oven to bake.

5. After it cools, you can have a slice of _____.

6. It will be _____ with a glass of milk.

TRY THIS! Make up a recipe for your favorite food. Write your recipe on a sheet of paper. Use as many Vocabulary Words as you can.

Practice Book
Just for You

© Harcourt

Name _____

| Skill Reminder | • **Proper nouns begin with a capital letter. Names of people are proper nouns.** |

• **Titles of people begin with a capital letter. Most titles are short forms of words. They often end with a period.**

▶ **Write each sentence. Use capital letters where they are needed.**

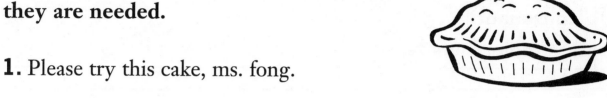

1. Please try this cake, ms. fong.

_____

2. My friend jody baked it.

_____

3. Doesn't mr. juarez like cake?

_____

4. Look out, octavio! _____
5. Thanks for helping claire and me.

_____

6. Did dr. jay bake this pie?

_____

7. Do sara, matt, and kwan want some more?

_____

8. billy ate all the cookies miss miller made.

_____

© Harcourt

Practice Book
Just for You

Name _____

Name _____

Syllable Rule

• **When two consonants come between two vowels in a word, divide after the first consonant.**
Example: pen/cil
• **When a two-syllable word with the VCCV pattern ends with -s, -es, or -ed, the word is still divided after the first consonant.**
Example: thun/dered

▶ Say each word. Then write the word with the endings. Listen to the number of syllables you hear. Then divide the word into syllables.

hammer
s   ed

1. _____hammered_____
2. _____hammers_____

question
s   ed

3. _____
4. _____

button
s   ed

5. _____
6. _____

enter
s   ed

7. _____
8. _____

© Harcourt

Name _____

▶ **Read the questions. Choose the answer that fits best. Fill in the circle next to your choice.**

1. Which word is a synonym for <u>alike</u>?

○ different   ○ same

○ funny   ○ about

💡 **Tip**
Synonyms are words with the same meaning.

2 Which word does *not* mean the same as <u>small</u>?

○ little   ○ tiny

○ petite   ○ big

💡 **Tip**
Make sure you read each question carefully.

3 Which word is a synonym for <u>noisy</u>?

○ quiet   ○ whisper

○ loud   ○ soft

Tip
Read all of the answer choices before making a decision.

© Harcourt

SCHOOL-HOME CONNECTION With your child, make a list of synonyms. Help your child use the synonyms in sentences.

73

Practice Book
Just for You

Name _____

▶ **Read the recipe. Then answer the questions.**

How to Make a Yummy Butter and Honey Sandwich

Things You Need

- 2 slices of bread
- 1 stick of butter
- 1 jar of honey
- plastic knife
- paper plate

Directions

1. Wash your hands before you touch the food.
2. Spread butter on the bread with a plastic knife.
3. Wash the knife in warm water.
4. Spread a little honey on the bread.
5. Put the slices of bread together.
6. Last, eat the sandwich.

1. What do you need to make the sandwich?
   - ○ salt, eggs, bread, knife, plate
   - ○ bread, jam, butter, knife, plate
   - ○ bread, butter, honey, knife, plate

💡 Tip
Read through the directions. Look for the list of the things you need.

2 What is the first thing you should do?
   - ○ Put the bread on a paper plate.
   - ○ Wash your hands.
   - ○ Spread honey on the bread.

3 What is the last thing you should do?
   - ○ Wash your hands.
   - ○ Butter the bread.
   - ○ Eat the sandwich.

💡 Tip
Following directions means following the steps in order.

© Harcourt

SCHOOL-HOME CONNECTION With your child, prepare a dish by following a recipe. Have your child help you by gathering and measuring ingredients. Help your child read the recipe.

Practice Book
Just for You

▶ **Circle the best answer to each riddle.**

1. This is the last month of the year.

         Apr.   **Nov.**   **Mar.**   **Dec.**

2. This is the first month of the year.

         Oct.   **Feb.**   **Dec.**   **Jan.**

3. This day comes after Saturday.

         Sun.   **Wed.**   **Fri.**   **Mon.**

4. This helps tell where someone lives.

         Mr.   **Nov.**   **Sat.**   **St.**

5. This day comes after Thursday.

         Tues.   **Fri.**   **Nov.**   **Wed.**

6. This is the day between Monday and Wednesday.

         Tues.   **Thurs.**   **Sat.**   **Sun.**

7. This person helps people who are sick.

         Dr.   **Mr.**   **St.**   **Dec.**

8. It is common to call a man this title.

         St.   **Dr.**   **Mr.**   **Mrs.**

9. This is a hot summer month.

         Jan.   **Aug.**   **Feb.**   **Dec.**

10. This is the title of a married woman.

         Mr.   **Mar.**   **St.**   **Mrs.**

© Harcourt

SCHOOL-HOME CONNECTION Make a list of
common abbreviations. Then have your child write
the longer word for each abbreviation.

75

Practice Book
Just for You

Name _____

▶ **Write the words from the box where they
belong in the chart. Make sure the words you
write have the same sound as the underlined letters.**

harm	sparkle	far	park	remark	alarm
charm	star	bar	jar	dark	farm

c<u>ar</u>	<u>arm</u>	b<u>ar</u>k

SCHOOL-HOME CONNECTION With your child,
make up rhymes using some of the words from
this lesson. Take turns adding to each other's
rhymes.

76

Practice Book
Just for You

▶ **Read the Spelling Words. Sort the words and write them where they belong.**

Spelling Words

Words with *ar*	Words with *ark*
1. _____	4. _____
2. _____	5. _____
3. _____	6. _____

Words with *arm*	
7. _____	9. _____
8. _____	10. _____

bar
jar
star
farm
harm
charm
dark
remark
sparkle
alarm
fourteen
source
between
enough
idea

▶ **Write the words that are left in alphabetical order.**

11. _____	14. _____
12. _____	15. _____
13. _____	

Name _____

► **Circle and write the word that best completes each sentence.**

1. We went for a walk

   in the _____.   **park   peak   pair**

2. My dog began to _____.   **beak   book   bark**

3. I tapped my mom on

   the _____.   **arm   ark   and**

4. We saw a girl with a

   _____ of lemonade.   **jig   jar   jag**

5. Mom made a _____
   that it looked good.   **remake   read   remark**

6. Can we get a

   fruit _____, too?   **bar   bark   ban**

7. The lemons were fresh

   from the _____.   **far   farm   fan**

8. I gave this lemonade a

   big _____.   **star   steer   still**

SCHOOL-HOME CONNECTION Work with your
child to make up an advertisement, either written
or oral, selling lemonade or some other product.
Use the phonics words from this lesson.

78

Practice Book
Just for You

© Harcourt

Name _____

▶ **Finish the story. On each line, write a word
from the box.**

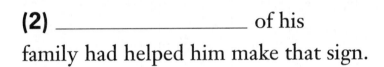

announced   arrived   glum   members   rebuild

"GET YOUR RED, RIPE APPLES
HERE!" Dan's sign

(1) _____. The

(2) _____ of his
family had helped him make that sign.

Oh, no! Look what Honey
did to Dan's stand!

Now he will have to **(3)** _____ it.

"Don't look so **(4)** _____,
Dan," said his mom. "We'll help you."

It's now as good as new. Someone

has **(5)** _____ to
buy some apples. Oh, no!
Here comes Honey again!

 TRY THIS! Write sentences about what you would like to sell at a stand.
Use Vocabulary Words in your sentences.

Practice Book
Just for You

Name _____

Skill Reminder • **Names of special animals begin
with a capital letter.**
• **Names of special places begin with a capital letter.**

▶ **Write each sentence. Use capital letters where they are
needed.**

1. Meet me at sun park. _____

2. It is on first street. _____

3. Bring your dogs, rex and tip.

_____

4. My dog, peppy, will be there.

_____

5. We can walk home along cherry lane.

_____

6. We'll stop to see andy and his cat, josie.

_____

7. They just moved here from salt lake city.

_____

 TRY THIS! Draw pictures of three pets you would like to have. Write a
name for each animal below its picture.

▶ **Find the word that has the same sound as the underlined letters in the first word. Fill in the circle next to your choice.**

Example: f<u>ar</u>

○ fare

○ care

○ mark

1 ch<u>ar</u>m

○ farm

○ share

○ fall

Tip
Read all the choices before you decide.

2 p<u>ar</u>k

○ tank

○ bake

○ sparkle

3 st<u>ar</u>light

○ darkness

○ stare

○ hear

Tip
Break a long word into syllables, and sound it out.

Name _____

▶ **Read the paragraph. Then complete the chart.**

Jen and Marco wanted to see the fish at the museum. Both worked to pay for the ticket. Jen sold drinks. Marco delivered newspapers. Jen worked alone. Marco worked with his brother. By Friday, both had earned $15. On Saturday, they went to the museum together!

Jen	Marco	Both
sold drinks. worked alone.	delivered newspapers. worked with his brother.	1. wanted to go to the museum. 2. _____. 3. _____. 4. _____.

SCHOOL-HOME CONNECTION Talk with your child about two family friends. Help your child write about one way the friends are alike and one way they are different.

82

Practice Book
Just for You

© Harcourt

Name _____

▶ **Look at the graph. Then answer the questions.
Fill in the circle next to the answer you choose.**

Number of cups of apple juice sold each week

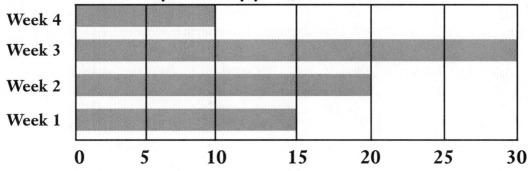

1 How many cups were
   sold in Week 1?

   ○ 20 cups

   ○ 10 cups

   ○ 15 cups

   Tip
   The numbers on the bottom of
   the chart show the number of
   cups sold.

2 In which week were
   20 cups sold?

   ○ Week 1

   ○ Week 2

   ○ Week 3

   Tip
   Remember, the
   length of the bar tells
   how many cups of
   apple juice were sold.

3 When was the most apple juice sold?

   ○ Week 4

   ○ Week 3

   ○ Week 2

   Tip
   Look for the longest
   bar.

SCHOOL-HOME CONNECTION Help your child
keep track of how many hours he or she sleeps each
night for four nights. Then work together to make a
bar graph like the one above to show this information.

83

Practice Book
Just for You

© Harcourt

Name _____

▶ **Circle the best answer to each riddle.**

1. It is where something comes from.   **source**   **stair**   **story**   **sold**

2. People play tennis on this.   **card**   **court**   **car**   **cord**

3. It is next after third.   **foot**   **fourth**   **felt**   **fold**

4. This comes after thirteen.   **far**   **first**   **fourteen**   **foot**

5. Sad people do this.   **moon**   **milk**   **more**   **mourn**

6. This is where cars race.   **corn**   **course**   **card**   **cold**

7. Sue did this to put milk into her glass.   **part**   **poured**   **pet**   **pig**

8. A book that gives information is this.   **read**   **rag**   **resource**   **red**

9. This is after three.   **form**   **farm**   **fire**   **four**

10. This belongs to you.   **yours**   **young**   **yellow**   **year**

© Harcourt

SCHOOL-HOME CONNECTION With your child, find five more words with the letters *our* and make up riddles.

84

Practice Book
Just for You

Name _____

▶ **Finish the story. On each line, write a word from the box.**

peers	deer	year	nearby
hear	cheers	pioneers	

Pioneer for a Year

Wouldn't it be fun to have been a pioneer for a

(1) _____? Imagine becoming friends with

animals like **(2)** _____. Can you

imagine having no stores **(3)** _____?

You would **(4)** _____ the sounds of

nature around you. I'm sure the lives of

(5) _____ were hard, too. There were

not many people around so they didn't have many

(6) _____. We should thank pioneers

with three loud **(7)** _____.

SCHOOL-HOME CONNECTION Work with your
child to create a diary page of what they think a
typical day would have been like for a pioneer.
Use words from this lesson in the diary entries.

85

© Harcourt

Practice Book
Just for You

▶ **Read the Spelling Words. Sort the words and write them where they belong.**

Words with *ear*	Words with *eer*
1. _____	6. _____
2. _____	7. _____
3. _____	8. _____
4. _____	9. _____
5. _____	10. _____

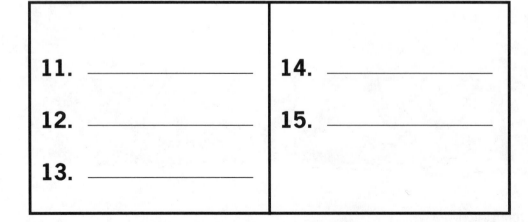

Spelling Words

pioneers
cheers
clearing
hear
nearby
year
beard
reindeer
steer
peer
remark
alarm
sleep
country
rain

▶ **Write the words that are left in alphabetical order.**

11. _____	14. _____
12. _____	15. _____
13. _____	

© Harcourt

Practice Book
Just for You

Name _____

▶ **Solve the riddles. Write a word from the box on each line.**

hear	year	deer	steer	beard
nearby	cheers	pioneers	peers	

1. You do this when you drive. You _____.

2. Men grow this on their chins. It's a _____.

3. This is twelve months. It's a _____.

4. You are not far away. You are _____.

5. This animal lives in the woods. It's a _____.

6. You do this with your ears. You _____.

7. People settled the land long ago.

They were _____.

8. Your classmates can be called this.

They are your _____.

9. Yells for a team are called this.

They are _____.

SCHOOL-HOME CONNECTION Work with your child to make crossword puzzle clues using words from this lesson. Extend the activity by making a crossword puzzle.

87

Practice Book
Just for You

© Harcourt

▶ **Complete the sentences. On each line, write a word from the box.**

frontier	nearby	orchards
survive	tame	wild

1. Rose and her family went out west to live on the

_____.

2. One day they passed by some apple _____.

3. Rose saw a yellow kitten hiding under a tree. She knew the

kitten couldn't _____ alone.

4. At first the kitten ran away from her like a

_____ animal.

5. Rose was sure she could

_____ the kitten.

6. Now wherever Rose goes,

the kitten is always _____.

Pretend that you are Rose. Write a letter to a friend telling about your trip out west. Use as many Vocabulary Words as you can.

Practice Book
Just for You

© Harcourt

Name _____

Skill Reminder • **The names of days of the week are proper nouns.**
• **The names of days begin with a capital letter.**

▶ **Write each sentence. Use capital letters where they are needed.**

1. We picked apples on sunday.

_____

2. On monday I took apples to school.

_____

3. We ate apples on tuesday.

_____

4. On wednesday we baked apple pies.

_____

5. We made apple butter on thursday.

_____

6. On friday we picked more apples.

_____

7. On saturday we ate more apples.

_____

8. On sunday I said, "No more apples!"

_____

© Harcourt

▶ **Find the word that has the same sound as the underlined letters in the first word. Fill in the circle next to your choice.**

Example: d<u>ee</u>r

      ○ dare

      ○ clear

      ○ hair

1 ch<u>ee</u>r

    ○ hear

    ○ chair

    ○ care

> **Tip**
> Sound out the words to yourself silently.

2 y<u>ear</u>ly

    ○ yawn

    ○ deer

    ○ heard

> **Tip**
> Read the whole word. Listen closely to the vowel sound.

3 engin<u>ee</u>r

    ○ fearless

    ○ parent

    ○ scare

> **Tip**
> Read each answer carefully.

© Harcourt

Name _____

▶ **Read the story. Then choose the best answer to each question. Fill in the circle next to your choice.**

Johnny's Hat

Johnny Appleseed sometimes wore a pot on his head. The pot was gray with a long handle. The handle was curved. Johnny wore the pot to keep his head dry. It fit his head just right.

1 Johnny's pot was

- ○ blue.
- ○ white.
- ○ black.
- ○ gray.

 Tip
As you read, watch for important details.

2 How did the pot fit Johnny's head?

- ○ The pot fit just right.
- ○ The pot was too small.
- ○ The pot was too big.
- ○ The pot was too heavy.

Tip
Reread the story to find the answer.

© Harcourt

SCHOOL-HOME CONNECTION With your child, talk about the clothing he or she is planning to wear to school tomorrow. Help your child write three sentences using details to describe the clothing.

Practice Book
Just for You

▶ **Write the words from the box that best complete the poem. Remember that the word you write should rhyme with the last word in the line above.**

far	charm	star	dark

Once I opened a covered jar.

Inside I found a big white

_____.

It was so bright, it lit up our farm.

It sparkled like a shiny

_____.

I took my star inside the car.

I took my star near and

_____.

I took my star to the park

Wherever I went, it was never

_____.

SCHOOL-HOME CONNECTION Help your child write a list of words with the phonograms *ar*, *arm*, and *ark*.

92

Practice Book
Just for You

© Harcourt

Name _____

▶ **Complete the sentences. Write each answer on the lines.**

1. Push the baby gently in the ___*stroller*___ .

    slide   **stroller**   **sweet**

2. My _____ is red and sore.

    table   **tea**   **throat**

3. Let's go swimming in the cool _____.

    stream   **swing**   **sap**

4. There are _____ people in my family.

    too   **tap**   **three**

5. Please don't _____ me with the hose!

    sock   **salad**   **spray**

6. The tree _____ new leaves.

    sung   **sprouted**   **space**

7. A _____ on my backpack broke.

    strap   **strong**   **story**

© Harcourt

SCHOOL-HOME CONNECTION Work with your child to write sentences using at least two words from this lesson in each sentence. Then have your child draw a picture that represents each sentence.

93

Name _____

▶ **Read the Spelling Words. Sort the words and write them where they belong.**

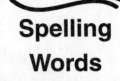

Spelling Words

sprout
streams
through
strong
strap
springtime
spray
throat
three
ostrich
pioneers
clearing
air
different
light

Words with *spr*	Words with *thr*
1. _____	4. _____
2. _____	5. _____
3. _____	6. _____

Words with *str*	
7. _____	9. _____
8. _____	10. _____

▶ **Write the words that are left in alphabetical order.**

11. _____	14. _____
12. _____	15. _____
13. _____	

Practice Book
Just for You

Name _____

▶ **Solve the riddles. Write a word from the box on each line.**

ostrich	sprout	three	streams	throat
sprays	through	strong	springtime	strap

1. This is how a plant starts out. It's a _____.

2. These flow through the mountains. They are

   _____.

3. This is the number before four. It's _____.

4. This is a large, funny-looking bird. It's an

   _____.

5. This is not over or under. It's _____.

6. People who can lift heavy things are this. They are

   _____.

7. A hose does this to water. It _____.

8. This is the front part of the neck. It's the _____.

9. This is the time of year when flowers bloom. It's

   _____.

10. This is a strip of leather or cloth. It's a _____.

SCHOOL-HOME CONNECTION Invite your child to
write a paragraph using the words in the box above.
When your child is finished, have him or her circle all
the *spr, str,* and *thr* words.

Practice Book
Just for You

© Harcourt

Name _____

► **Finish the ad. On each line, write a word from the box.**

| beautiful | nutrition | protects | ripens | streams |

BEST SEED COMPANY

We sell seeds that grow into _____

plants. You can watch as the fruit of each plant

_____ in the fall. Many plants are part of good

_____, and they taste good, too!

You can use water from _____ to help your

seeds grow into strong plants. Think about building a fence.

A fence _____ your plants from hungry animals.
Send for your seeds today!

Best Seed Company
1414 Petal Place
Green City, TX 79909

TRY THIS! Write three sentences about a plant you would like to grow.
Use some of the Vocabulary Words in your sentences.

© Harcourt

Practice Book
Just for You

Name _____

Skill Reminder • **The names of the months are proper nouns.**

• **The names of the months begin with a capital letter.**

▶ **Write each sentence. Use capital letters where they are needed.**

1. We planted the seeds in january.

_____

2. We waited in february.

_____

3. In march we saw green stems.

_____

4. The plants grew big in april and may.

_____

_____

5. In june and july we had flowers.

_____

6. Can we plant again in september or october?

_____

_____

© Harcourt

Practice Book
Just for You

| Syllable Rule | • **When a single consonant is between two vowels, divide before the consonant. Try the first syllable long. If the word makes sense, keep it!** |

Examples: ti/ger   pa/per

• **If the word doesn't make sense, divide after the consonant and try it short.**

Examples: drag/on   vis/it

▶ Read the words on the left. Then write the words in syllables on the lines.

river   1. _____

travel   2. _____

polar   3. _____

palace   4. _____

broken   5. _____

hotel   6. _____

wagon   7. _____

freezer   8. _____

token   9. _____

ever   10. _____

Practice Book
Just for You

Name _____

▶ **Read the paragraph and the diagram. Then choose the best answer to each question. Fill in the circle next to your choice.**

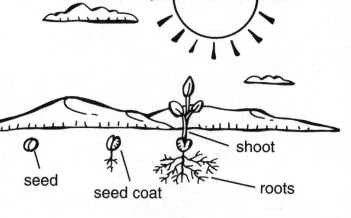

Germination

A new plant grows from a seed. The sun warms the seed in the ground. Then the seed coat breaks. Roots begin to grow down into the soil. The seed begins to sprout.

1 What does the diagram tell you?

○ the name of the new plant

○ the kind of soil

○ how a seed grows

○ the names of insects on plants

Tip
Remember to read all the information. Then choose your answer.

2 Use the diagram to help you. Which sentence would go best at the end of the paragraph?

○ Seeds look like small grains or nuts.

○ A shoot and leaves grow up toward the sun.

○ Insects feed on plants.

○ Plants have many leaves.

Tip
Choose a sentence that completes the paragraph.

SCHOOL-HOME CONNECTION Find a simple diagram in an instruction manual. Look at the diagram with your child. Then have him or her explain what is being shown in the diagram.

Practice Book
Just for You

Name _____

► **Circle the best answer to each riddle.**

1. You do this when
you drive.   **steer   step   stick   star**

2. This animal lives
where it's cold.   **rain   reindeer   rare   ready**

3. This is 365 days.   **yarn   yes   year   your**

4. This is what you do
with your ears.   **heat   hear   head   heal**

5. These people settled
in new places.   **pioneers   princes   pines   parts**

6. "Go, Team!"
is one of these.   **cheese   chest   charm   cheers**

7. This grows on
men's chins.   **bead   beard   belt   beam**

8. This is something
that is close.   **need   new   nearby   neat**

SCHOOL-HOME CONNECTION Have your child
choose a word from the lesson. Then ask your child
yes or no questions that lead you to guess the word.
Take turns guessing more words.

100

Practice Book
Just for You

© Harcourt

▶ **Write a word from the box on each line to
complete the sentences.**

roots	food	roof
room	pool	school

1. The moon rose over the _____.

2. I need a spoon to eat my _____.

3. There are five windows in this _____.

4. That plant has _____.

5. I went swimming in the _____.

6. In _____, I am in the second grade.

SCHOOL-HOME CONNECTION Ask your child to
draw and label pictures of the words *baboon*,
cartoon, and *boot*.

Practice Book
Just for You

▶ **Read the Spelling Words. Write each word where it belongs.**

Words with *oo*	
1. _____	6. _____
2. _____	7. _____
3. _____	8. _____
4. _____	9. _____
5. _____	10. _____

**Spelling
Words**

smooth
roots
food
scooter
boot
broom
moon
cartoon
roof
spoon
springtime
ostrich
answer
paper
page

▶ **Write the words that are left in alphabetical order.**

11. _____	14. _____
12. _____	15. _____
13. _____	

Practice Book
Just for You

Name _____

▶ **Circle and write the word that completes each
sentence.**

1. Mom packed some _____.
     food   foot   fool

2. I put on my hiking _____.
     boots   boats   boom

3. I jumped on my _____.
     scout   scoop   scooter

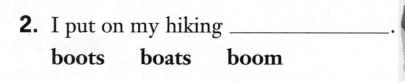

4. It's not a day to watch _____.
     car   cartoons   tools

5. I sat under a tree with _____ leaves.
     smock   spool   smooth

6. The tree had big _____.
     roots   room   road

7. I cleared a spot with my _____.
     bright   broom   book

8. I ate a snack with my _____.
     spool   spook   spoon

© Harcourt

SCHOOL-HOME CONNECTION Ask your child to
choose five words from this lesson and write
or tell a story using those five words.

103

Practice Book
Just for You

▶ **Complete the sentences. On each line, write a word from the box.**

discover	energy	forecast	shed	source

1. Before we hike, we listen to the weather

_____.

2. If it is going to be a sunny day, we

_____ our sneakers

and put on our hiking boots.

3. We eat a picnic lunch to give us

_____ for a

long walk.

4. It is fun to _____
the ways animals use trees to make
their homes.

5. The trees are also a good

_____ of food

for them.

TRY THIS! Draw a picture of rainy weather, sunny weather, and snowy weather. Write a sentence about each picture using as many Vocabulary Words as possible.

Name _____

Skill Reminder • **Important words in the names of holidays begin with a capital letter.**

▶ Match the holidays with the picture clues. Write a holiday name from the box on each line. Use capital letters where they are needed.

| valentine's day | fourth of july | thanksgiving |
| groundhog day | mother's day | presidents' day |

1. _____

2. _____

3. _____

4. _____

5. _____

6. _____

 TRY THIS! Draw a picture that shows what you do during your favorite holiday. Write two sentences to go with your picture. Use the name of the holiday at least once.

© Harcourt

Practice Book
Just for You

Name _____

Syllable Rule	• **When a word ends in a**

**consonant and _le_, divide the word before the
consonant.**
Example: cir/cle

▶ Read the words in the box. Write each word in syllables
where it belongs in the chart. Cross out each word in the
box after you write it.

able	babble	bridle	candle	cycle
fable	rattle	saddle	title	uncle

ta/ble

1. _____

2. _____

3. _____

4. _____

5. _____

rip/ple

6. _____

7. _____

8. _____

9. _____

10. _____

Name _____

▶ **Read the book titles and their descriptions. Then fill in the circle that best answers each question.**

Trees and Their Leaves
by
Maya Moorely

This book describes how leaves change color in the fall.

The Tree That Could Talk
by
Steve West

This book tells of a tree that can talk when fed purple water.

Guide to Trees
by
José Runello

This book gives information on how to identify trees by their leaves.

1 Which book is fiction? ————

○ *Trees and Their Leaves*

○ *The Tree That Could Talk*

○ *Guide to Trees*

○ None of the above

 Tip
Fiction often includes events that could not happen in real life.

2 Which book is fact? ————

○ *Trees and Their Leaves*

○ *The Tree That Could Talk*

○ *Guide to Trees*

○ Both *Trees and Their Leaves* and *Guide to Trees*

Tip
When an answer has the word *both*, make sure that both items fit the question.

© Harcourt

SCHOOL-HOME CONNECTION Read excerpts from a newspaper article and a fairy tale to your child. Have him or her tell you which is fact and which is fiction. Then have your child explain why.

Practice Book
Just for You

Name _____

▶ **Write the words from the box that best
complete the poem. Remember that the word
you write should rhyme with the last word in the line above.**

strong	stream	sprout	strap	through	springtime

Once I had a crazy dream

that I was boating in a _____.

In my boat I had a cat with a cap

and a puppy on a _____.

The sky was blue and the sun did shine

because it was beautiful _____.

We hummed and sang a happy song

My puppy rowed 'cause he is _____.

In the stream we saw a trout,

and in the grass a little _____.

My friends and I know just what to do.

We'll row and sing the whole day _____.

SCHOOL-HOME CONNECTION Invite your child
to make up a short story including the words *sprout*,
streams, *three*, and *springtime*.   **108**

Practice Book
Just for You

© Harcourt

Name _____

▶ **Read each sentence. Choose the word with _gn_, _kn_, or _wr_ that sounds like _gnome_, _knee_, or _write_.**

1. There is a _____ in the rope

   knot   tear   rip

2. My _____ is broken.

   arm   hand   wrist

3. The _____ flew in the house.

   gnat   bee   fly

4. You need a _____ to cut your steak.

   fork   knife   spoon

5. I have to _____ a story.

   hear   tell   write

SCHOOL-HOME CONNECTION List some of the words from this lesson on a sheet of paper. Ask your child to cover the silent letter in each word.   **109**

Practice Book
Just for You

© Harcourt

Name _____

▶ **Read the Spelling Words. Sort the words and write them where they belong.**

Words with *gn*	
1. _____	2. _____

Words with *kn*	Words with *wr*
3. _____	7. _____
4. _____	8. _____
5. _____	9. _____
6. _____	10. _____

Spelling Words

knock
knew
knight
wrong
write
sign
gnat
wrist
unknown
writer
scooter
cartoon
dark
front
past

▶ **Sort the words that are left by the number of syllables.**

One-Syllable Words	Two-Syllable Words
11. _____	14. _____
12. _____	15. _____
13. _____	

© Harcourt

Name _____

▶ **Solve the riddles. Write a word from the box
on each line.**

wrong	knock	wrist	knew
gnat	writer	write	sign

1. She's a person who writes books. She's a _____.

2. This can be posted as a warning. It's a _____.

3. This is not right. It's _____.

4. This is a tiny insect. It's a _____.

5. This is part of your arm. It's your _____.

6. When you tap on a door, you do this. You

   _____.

7. When you make words on paper, you do this.

   You _____.

8. When you know the answer,
   you can say this.

   I _____ that!

SCHOOL-HOME CONNECTION Ask your child to
look up in a dictionary or think of three more words
beginning with *gn*, *kn*, or *wr*. Ask your child to think
of a riddle for each of these words.

Practice Book
Just for You

© Harcourt

▶ **Complete the picture labels to tell what Chris's family did when company came. On each line, write a term from the box.**

| beneath | relay race | shimmered | snug | wrinkled | knelt |

I put on shorts that were clean and

not _____.

We _____ on the ground to
play with my truck.

We ran a _____ together.

We sat _____ a big tree
to eat lunch.

The lake _____ in
the sun when we went for a swim.

My brother took a nap, _____
in Grandma's lap.

TRY THIS! Write a few sentences about a summer activity you like. Use as many Vocabulary Words as you can.

© Harcourt

Name _____

Watermelon Day
Grammar:
Abbreviations

Skill Reminder • **The names of the months are proper nouns.**

• **The names of the months begin with a capital letter.**

▶ **Write the abbreviation for each month or day. Add capital letters and periods to the abbreviations in ( ).**

the abbreviation for **January**	_____	(jan)
the abbreviation for **February**	_____	(feb)
the abbreviation for **August**	_____	(aug)
the abbreviation for **September**	_____	(sept)
the abbreviation for **November**	_____	(nov)
the abbreviation for **Monday**	_____	(mon)
the abbreviation for **Wednesday**	_____	(wed)
the abbreviation for **Friday**	_____	(fri)

AUGUST						
S	M	T	W	T	F	S
		1	2	3	4	5
6	7	8	9	10	11	12
13	14	15	16	17	18	19
20	21	22	23	24	25	26
27	28	29	30	31		

TRY THIS! Write a list telling something you like to do on each of the seven days of the week. Use abbreviations for the names of days. For example, Mon.—play baseball.

© Harcourt

113

Practice Book
Just for You

Skill Reminder • **When a word ends in consonant and -*le*, divide the word before the consonant.**
• **When a word with consonant and -*le* adds -*ed*, it changes spelling. The ending becomes part of the second syllable.**

▶ Read the words in the box. Write each word in syllables where it belongs.

wrinkled	tangle	giggled	sparkled	circled

Words with Consonant and -*le*	Words with Consonant and -*le* + -*ed*
1. sparkle	_____
2. giggle	_____
3. _____	tangled
4. circle	_____
5. wrinkle	_____

Practice Book
Just for You

▶ **Read the paragraph. Then choose the best answer to each question. Fill in the circle next to your choice.**

Sammy walked around the corner. He saw *ten* watermelons in a row. He also saw peaches across from the watermelons. A man with an apron was stacking the peaches on a shelf. Then Sammy heard his father call his name. He ran to join his father at the check-out counter.

1 This story most likely takes place

- ○ at Sammy's house.
- ○ at school.
- ○ at the beach.
- ○ at the grocery store.

 Tip
Reread the paragraph to make sure you know the details.

2 It is most likely that Sammy is

- ○ walking home from school.
- ○ buying food with his father.
- ○ walking on the beach.
- ○ on vacation.

Tip
Look for clue words in the story to help you make inferences.

SCHOOL-HOME CONNECTION Read a few sentences from a travel brochure or guide with your child. Help your child look for clue words to make inferences about the place being described.

115

Practice Book
Just for You

© Harcourt

Name _____

▶ **Circle the best answer to each riddle.**

1. This is what you do when you practice.
remark   remake   rehearse   real

2. This is not late. It is this.
early   each   eagle   eel

3. This is what you do in school to gain knowledge.
learn   lean   leak   leaf

4. This is where you plant flowers.
each   eight   earth   earn

5. This comes from an oyster.
pear   pail   pour   pearl

6. This is what you do when you look for something.
sea   search   seam   seed

7. When you work for money you do this.
elm   empty   earn   early

© Harcourt

SCHOOL-HOME CONNECTION Go on a word hunt with your child. Look through magazines, books, and newspapers for words from this exercise. Write them down and count how many you find.

116

Practice Book
Just for You

▶ **Finish the story. On each line, write a word from the box.**

babies	duties	skies
cries	cities	pennies

The Contest

The **(1)** _____ of Appleville and Bananaville

hold a strange contest. They gather all their

(2) _____ under the bright, sunny

(3) _____ to see who **(4)** _____

the loudest. People put **(5)** _____ in jars to

vote for the loudest baby. The mayor called, "We have to count

the money. Please do your **(6)** _____ quickly.

This is too loud! Let's have a different contest next year.

Something quieter!"

SCHOOL-HOME CONNECTION Look at the
words from this lesson. Discuss with your child
how the spelling of these words changes, for
example from one *baby* to several *babies*.

117

Practice Book
Just for You

© Harcourt

▶ **Read the Spelling Words. Write the words where they belong.**

Words With *ies*	
1. _____	6. _____
2. _____	7. _____
3. _____	8. _____
4. _____	9. _____
5. _____	10. _____

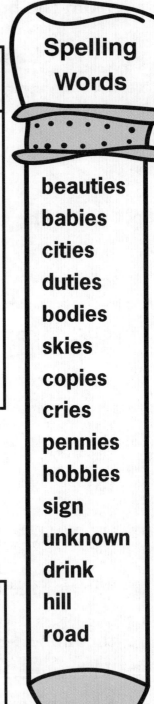

Spelling Words

beauties
babies
cities
duties
bodies
skies
copies
cries
pennies
hobbies
sign
unknown
drink
hill
road

▶ **Write the words that are left in alphabetical order.**

11. _____	14. _____
12. _____	15. _____
13. _____	

© Harcourt

Practice Book
Just for You

Name _____

▶ **Solve the riddles. Write a word from the box on each line.**

cries	skies	cities	hobbies
babies	pennies	copies	duties

1. These are one-cent coins. They are _____.

2. Stamp-collecting and postcard-collecting are types of these.

   They are _____.

3. The baby does this when he is sad. He _____.

4. The teacher needs more than one worksheet. She

   makes _____.

5. This word means "more than one sky." It is

   _____.

6. These are things people have to do. They are

   _____.

7. These places are bigger than towns.

   They are _____.

8. Newborns are called this. They are _____.

SCHOOL-HOME CONNECTION Ask your child to list five words that end with *y*. Work with him or her to change these words to their plural forms.

119

Practice Book
Just for You

© Harcourt

► **Complete each sentence in the story with a
Vocabulary Word from the box.**

boasted	crept	crown	village	vines

The Sneaky Monkey

The sneaky monkey wanted to wear the king's

_____. He swung on _____ until he made it

through the forest. Then the monkey _____ along on

the ground. He snuck around the houses in the _____

to find the king's castle. The monkey put the crown on his head.

Later he _____ to the other animals, "I am the king of
the jungle!"

 TRY THIS! Think about the different fruits and flowers that grow on vines.
Write sentences about them. Use as many Vocabulary Words
as you can.

Harcourt

Name _____

Skill Reminder • **A possessive noun tells what someone or something owns or has. When a possessive noun names one person or thing, add an apostrophe (') and s to show ownership.**

▶ **Finish each sentence. Change the noun in ( ) to show ownership, and write it on the line.**

1. We all sit in _____ garden. **(Ben)**

2. _____ little brother holds some seeds. **(Myrna)**

3. _____ mom teaches us about planting. **(Vin)**

4. _____ dog barks. **(Pam)**

5. Where is the _____ bone? **(dog)**

6. Is it under the _____ flowers? **(girl)**

7. No, it is under that _____ foot. **(boy)**

8. Here comes _____ sister with water for the plants! **(Pete)**

TRY THIS! Write three sentences about things that belong to people you know. In each sentence, use the name of a person. Add an apostrophe and s to show ownership.

© Harcourt

Name _____

▶ **Find the word that is spelled correctly. Fill in the circle next to the answer you choose.**

Example cherry

   ○ cherrys

   ○ cherries

   ○ cherryes

1 sleep

> **Tip**
> Say the choices aloud. Which one sounds correct?

   ○ sleepes

   ○ sleepies

   ○ sleeps

2 wash

   ○ washs

   ○ washes

   ○ washies

3 belly

> **Tip**
> Look at the letter before the y. Remember the rule for adding –s to a word that ends with in y.

   ○ bellies

   ○ bellys

   ○ bellyes

© Harcourt

Practice Book
Just for You

Name _____

▶ **Here is how Mack began a letter. Read it and think about what happens next. Then answer each question.**

Dear Grandma,

Do you remember the carrot seeds you sent us? Mom and I planted them in our garden. We watered them a lot. You told me to talk to them. I said, "Grow, carrots. Grow!" I checked those carrot seeds every day for weeks. Nothing happened. I wanted to tell you, "Those seeds are no good." Then, this morning something happened. You won't believe what I found.

1. What do you think Mack found?

💡 **Tip**
Reread the paragraph for clues.

_____

2. What story clues helped you predict what happened?

💡 **Tip**
Think about what is being described.

_____

_____

3. Do you think Mack will tell his mother? _____

💡 **Tip**
Think about how Mack feels.

SCHOOL-HOME CONNECTION Work with your child to make up the first part of a story about an unusual plant. Talk about what might happen at the end. Then ask your child to tell you an ending for the story.

123

Practice Book
Just for You

© Harcourt

Name _____

▶ **Read the story. Write the words with *our* on the lines.**

four	poured	course	court	fourteen	source

My sister is four years old. I am in fourth grade. We wanted to build a sand castle together. First, we needed a source for the sand. We went to the beach and poured sand into our buckets. We built a large castle. It had a court made of seashells and a moat. Of course, the water came up later and washed the castle away. We still had a great day.

1. _____

2. _____

3. _____

4. _____

5. _____

6. _____

© Harcourt

SCHOOL-HOME CONNECTION Explain the difference between the number *four* and the word *fourth* to your child. Look for other examples of written numbers and their ordinals (*first, second, third,* etc.).

Practice Book
Just for You

Skills and Strategies Index

COMPREHENSION

Alphabetical order 49

Author's purpose 16

Compare and contrast 32, 82

Details 91

Fact and Fiction 107

Follow two-step written
directions 74

Important information
Charts and graphs 83
Reading diagrams 99

Locate information 8

Main idea 7, 57

Make inferences 115

Narrative elements 24, 40

Predict outcomes 65, 123

PHONICS/DECODING

Common Abbreviations 59, 61, 64,
75

Consonant Blends: *spr, str, thr* 93,
95, 108

Consonant Digraphs
/n/ *gn, kn,* /r/ *wr* 109, 111

Nouns and verbs with and without
inflectional endings
-ed 18, 20, 23, 31, 33
-ed (y to I) 26, 28, 41
-s, -es, -ies (y to I) 117, 119, 122

Phonograms
-ack, -ock 42, 44, 58
-ame, -ake 10, 12, 15, 25
-ar, -arm, -ark 76, 78, 81
-at, -ate 34, 36, 50
-id, ide 1, 3, 9, 17

R-Controlled Vowels
/ir/ *ear, eer* 85, 87, 90, 92, 100
/ôr/ *our* 67, 69, 84, 124
/ûr/ *ear* 51, 53, 66, 116

Syllable Pattern
c-le 106, 114
compound words 39
VCCV 47, 56
VCCV with endings 72
VCV 98

Syllables 6

Vowel Digraphs
/o͞o/ *oo* 101, 103

Skills and Strategies Index

GRAMMAR

SPELLING

VOCABULARY

· T R O P H I E S ·

End-of-Selection Tests

Grade 2-1

The Mixed-Up Chameleon

Directions: For items 1–18, fill in the circle in front of the correct answer. For items 19–20, write the answer.

Vocabulary

1. We _____ a red bird up in the tree.
Ⓐ handsome   Ⓑ hardly
Ⓒ spotted   Ⓓ clustered

2. The girl's ring was _____ gold.
Ⓐ sideways   Ⓑ sparkling
Ⓒ excited   Ⓓ fishing

3. We could _____ see the sun behind the clouds.
Ⓐ hardly   Ⓑ handsome
Ⓒ dull   Ⓓ spotted

4. The paint on the old bike is _____.
Ⓐ hardly   Ⓑ pride
Ⓒ hungry   Ⓓ dull

5. A very good-looking man is _____.
Ⓐ handsome   Ⓑ sideways
Ⓒ spotted   Ⓓ sparkling

6. This story is interesting and _____.
Ⓐ hardly   Ⓑ spotted
Ⓒ dull   Ⓓ exciting

Practice Book
Just for You

7. A chameleon can move its eyes _____.

   Ⓐ exciting   Ⓑ spotted

   Ⓒ sideways   Ⓓ handsome

Comprehension

8. This story is most like a _____.

   Ⓐ science book   Ⓑ true story

   Ⓒ fantasy story   Ⓓ folktale

9. At the beginning of the story, what happens when the chameleon moves from one thing to another?

   Ⓐ The chameleon changes its shape to match the thing's shape.

   Ⓑ The chameleon changes its color to match what it is on.

   Ⓒ The chameleon changes into another animal.

   Ⓓ The chameleon moves its eyes in a different way.

10. When does the chameleon turn sparkling green?

   Ⓐ when it is cold and hungry

   Ⓑ when it goes to sleep

   Ⓒ when it is warm and full

   Ⓓ when it changes into a polar bear

Practice Book
Just for You

11. When does the chameleon turn gray and dull?

(A) when the weather is rainy

(B) when it is cold and hungry

(C) when it is not on a leaf

(D) when it is nighttime

12. What do chameleons eat?

(A) leaves   (B) birds

(C) worms   (D) flies

13. How does a chameleon catch its food?

(A) with its long, sticky tongue

(B) with its sharp claws

(C) with its sticky lips

(D) with its long tail

14. When the chameleon sees the animals in the zoo, how does it feel about itself?

(A) pleased   (B) proud

(C) bad   (D) so-so

15. What is the first animal at the zoo that the chameleon wants to be like?

(A) a flamingo   (B) a fox

(C) a fish   (D) a polar bear

Grade 2-1

© Harcourt

Practice Book
Just for You

16. The chameleon wishes to be like a flamingo because a flamingo _____.

Ⓐ is pink   Ⓑ sees far away

Ⓒ is handsome   Ⓓ can run fast

17. Why does the chameleon make its last wish?

Ⓐ It wants to be beautiful.

Ⓑ It is hungry.

Ⓒ It wants an exciting life.

Ⓓ A fly is teasing it.

18. What does the chameleon learn is best for itself?

Ⓐ being a chameleon   Ⓑ being strong

Ⓒ being funny   Ⓓ being a fly

19. The title of the story is "The Mixed-Up Chameleon." *Mixed up* has two meanings. How does the chameleon get mixed up in how it looks?

_____

_____

_____

20. Why is the chameleon mixed up about how to catch the fly?

_____

_____

_____

Practice Book
Just for You

Get Up and Go!

Directions: For items 1–18, fill in the circle in front of the correct answer. For items 19–20, write the answer.

Vocabulary

1. There are 60 _____ in an hour.
  Ⓐ always   Ⓑ snuggle
  Ⓒ names   Ⓓ minutes

2. She is _____ the last to go.
  Ⓐ always   Ⓑ take
  Ⓒ treat   Ⓓ time

3. We don't have _____ on Friday night.
  Ⓐ always   Ⓑ homework
  Ⓒ minutes   Ⓓ ready

4. My dog gets a _____ every night.
  Ⓐ same   Ⓑ homework
  Ⓒ treat   Ⓓ late

5. My cats like to _____ next to me.
  Ⓐ snuggle   Ⓑ minutes
  Ⓒ always   Ⓓ slow

Practice Book
Just for You

Comprehension

6. This story is mostly about how a little girl _____.

Ⓐ washes her face

Ⓑ plays with her dog

Ⓒ gets ready for school

Ⓓ rides the school bus

7. The little girl can wash her face in _____.

Ⓐ 3 minutes   Ⓑ 8 minutes

Ⓒ 10 minutes   Ⓓ 15 minutes

8. The story takes place in the little girl's _____.

Ⓐ school   Ⓑ bus

Ⓒ home   Ⓓ bed

9. What is the name of the dog in the story?

Ⓐ Sammie   Ⓑ Snack

Ⓒ Dog   Ⓓ Go

10. What is the last thing the girl does as she leaves?

Ⓐ hugs   Ⓑ washes

Ⓒ packs   Ⓓ eats

11. What is the dog's favorite meal?

Ⓐ snack time   Ⓑ lunch

Ⓒ breakfast   Ⓓ dinner

12. What does the girl like to do in the morning?
- Ⓐ get out of bed
- Ⓑ stay in bed
- Ⓒ be late
- Ⓓ hurry up

13. The girl takes six minutes to _____.
- Ⓐ brush her teeth and hair
- Ⓑ give the dog a treat
- Ⓒ run downstairs
- Ⓓ do homework

14. What is the total time the little girl takes to get ready for school?
- Ⓐ 5 minutes
- Ⓑ 8 minutes
- Ⓒ 36 minutes
- Ⓓ 6 hours

15. What does the dog wish the girl would do?
- Ⓐ snuggle Teddy longer
- Ⓑ share her toast
- Ⓒ brush her teeth
- Ⓓ play games with him

16. The dog checks up on the girl because she is _____.
- Ⓐ playing a game
- Ⓑ brushing her teeth
- Ⓒ taking too long
- Ⓓ riding the bus

Grade 2-1

Practice Book
Just for You

17. When Sammie puts all the time lines together,
he is _____.
(A) adding   (B) subtracting
(C) multiplying   (D) resting

18. This book is most like a _____.
(A) fairy tale   (B) play
(C) story book   (D) biography

19. Why is "Get Up and Go!" a good title for the story?

_____

_____

_____

_____

_____

20. What does Sammie mean when he says, "The rest of
the day is totally mine"?

_____

_____

_____

_____

_____

Practice Book
Just for You

Henry and Mudge Under the Yellow Moon

Directions: For items 1–18, fill in the circle in front of the correct answer. For items 19–20, write the answer.

Vocabulary

1. We saw some _____ eating nuts.
Ⓐ woods
Ⓑ south
Ⓒ chipmunks
Ⓓ handsome

2. We _____ flowers to give to Mother.
Ⓐ barked
Ⓑ picked
Ⓒ woods
Ⓓ helped

3. Many birds fly _____ in the winter.
Ⓐ sniffing
Ⓑ woods
Ⓒ picked
Ⓓ south

4. My dog is _____ for a bone.
Ⓐ sniffing
Ⓑ finished
Ⓒ south
Ⓓ eating

5. Many trees grow in the _____.
Ⓐ picked
Ⓑ car
Ⓒ woods
Ⓓ leaves

Practice Book
Just for You

Grade 2-1

Comprehension

6. This story is most like a _____.
Ⓐ fable   Ⓑ play
Ⓒ true story   Ⓓ fiction story

7. Mudge is a _____.
Ⓐ boy   Ⓑ cat
Ⓒ dog   Ⓓ bird

8. Henry likes to count birds. Mudge likes to _____.
Ⓐ look for chipmunks
Ⓑ pick apples
Ⓒ fly south
Ⓓ eat leaves

9. When does this story take place?
Ⓐ in the spring   Ⓑ in the summer
Ⓒ in the fall   Ⓓ in the winter

10. Who are Henry and Mudge?
Ⓐ two boys   Ⓑ a boy and a dog
Ⓒ a dog and a cat   Ⓓ two dogs

11. Henry and Mudge like to _____.
Ⓐ walk in the woods together
Ⓑ pick apples together
Ⓒ walk to town together
Ⓓ go bird-watching together

12. Henry looks at the trees because the _____.

Ⓐ trees are full of birds

Ⓑ leaves are pretty colors

Ⓒ wind blows the leaves

Ⓓ trees are full of apples

13. Henry looks at the tops of the trees, but Mudge _____.

Ⓐ sniffs the ground

Ⓑ sits at the foot of a tree

Ⓒ sleeps under a bush

Ⓓ counts the birds flying south

14. In the fall, the leaves turn _____.

Ⓐ north and south   Ⓑ orange and yellow

Ⓒ inside out   Ⓓ to apples

15. What interests Mudge most?

Ⓐ leaves   Ⓑ birds

Ⓒ being with Henry   Ⓓ apples

16. What does Mudge do with apples?

Ⓐ He licks them.   Ⓑ He eats them.

Ⓒ He sniffs them.   Ⓓ He cooks them.

17. More than anything else, Henry and Mudge like to _____.

Ⓐ look at the leaves   Ⓑ eat apples

Ⓒ walk in the woods   Ⓓ be together

18. This story is mostly about _____.
- Ⓐ a boy walking in the woods
- Ⓑ a dog eating leaves
- Ⓒ a boy and his dog being friends
- Ⓓ a boy and his dog playing together

19. Henry and Mudge do things differently because

_____

_____

_____

_____

_____

_____

20. How are Henry's coat and Mudge's coat different?

_____

_____

_____

_____

_____

_____

Practice Book
Just for You

Days With Frog and Toad

Directions: For items 1–18, fill in the circle in front of the correct answer. For items 19–20, write the answer.

Vocabulary

1. We gave our sick friend a book to _____ her up.
- Ⓐ alone
- Ⓑ cheer
- Ⓒ spoiled
- Ⓓ wonder

2. Sometimes I play with friends, but other times I play _____.
- Ⓐ alone
- Ⓑ cheer
- Ⓒ reason
- Ⓓ send

3. Grass and flowers grow in the _____.
- Ⓐ alone
- Ⓑ spoiled
- Ⓒ cheer
- Ⓓ meadow

4. He was sick, but now he is _____.
- Ⓐ reason
- Ⓑ cheer
- Ⓒ fine
- Ⓓ basket

5. Do you have a good _____ for being late?
- Ⓐ reason
- Ⓑ spoiled
- Ⓒ fine
- Ⓓ hurried

6. The rain _____ our fun at the park.
- Ⓐ alone
- Ⓑ fine
- Ⓒ cheer
- Ⓓ spoiled

Practice Book
Just for You

Grade 2-1

Comprehension

7. What is this story mostly about?

Ⓐ Turtle carrying Toad to the island

Ⓑ Toad falling into the river

Ⓒ Frog being very sad

Ⓓ Toad being a good friend to Frog

8. The story takes place mostly _____.

Ⓐ on an island   Ⓑ in a meadow

Ⓒ in Frog's house   Ⓓ on a boat

9. When Toad first reads Frog's note, Toad feels _____.

Ⓐ puzzled   Ⓑ scared

Ⓒ sad   Ⓓ happy

10. When Toad finds Frog, Frog is _____.

Ⓐ swimming in the river

Ⓑ sitting on an island

Ⓒ walking through a meadow

Ⓓ resting in the woods

11. Why does Toad make a picnic lunch?

Ⓐ Toad is suddenly hungry.

Ⓑ Frog asks Toad to make lunch.

Ⓒ Toad wants to eat lunch with Turtle.

Ⓓ Toad wants to make Frog happy.

12. Toad shouts and waves at Frog. Why doesn't Frog answer?

(A) Frog is too sad to speak to Toad.

(B) Frog is mad at Toad.

(C) Frog doesn't see or hear Toad.

(D) Frog is talking to Turtle.

13. How does Toad get to the island where Frog is?

(A) Toad swims to the island.

(B) Toad rides on a turtle's back.

(C) Frog swims and pulls Toad.

(D) Toad takes a boat.

14. Why does the turtle think that Toad should leave Frog alone?

(A) The turtle knows that Frog is not at home.

(B) The island is too small for the two friends.

(C) Frog wrote a note saying he wants to be alone.

(D) The sun is shining.

15. Why does Toad tell Frog that he is sorry?

(A) Toad gets Frog wet when he slips off the turtle.

(B) Toad forgets to bring lunch.

(C) Toad thinks, "Maybe Frog thinks that I am silly and dumb."

(D) Their lunch is spoiled.

Practice Book
Just for You

16. Lunch spoils because _____.
  Ⓐ Toad leaves it at home
  Ⓑ the iced tea spills on the sandwiches
  Ⓒ it gets too warm
  Ⓓ it falls into the river

17. When Frog sees Toad, Frog is _____.
  Ⓐ mad that Toad has not left him alone
  Ⓑ sad that lunch is spoiled
  Ⓒ happy to see his friend
  Ⓓ afraid that Toad will stay too long

18. What do Frog and Toad eat for lunch?
  Ⓐ wet sandwiches without iced tea
  Ⓑ wet sandwiches with iced tea
  Ⓒ dry sandwiches without iced tea
  Ⓓ dry sandwiches with iced tea

19. Name one reason why Frog is happy.

_____

_____

_____

20. Why had Frog wanted to be alone?

_____

_____

_____

Practice Book
Just for You

Wilson Sat Alone

Directions: For items 1–18, fill in the circle in front of the correct answer. For items 19–20, write the answer.

Vocabulary

1. Ted and Maria _____ up the hill.
- Ⓐ raced
- Ⓑ thanked
- Ⓒ amazing
- Ⓓ opened

2. The girls _____ in one room to sing.
- Ⓐ amazing
- Ⓑ gathered
- Ⓒ remarked
- Ⓓ named

3. It was _____ to see what happened.
- Ⓐ wandered
- Ⓑ clustered
- Ⓒ amazing
- Ⓓ raced

4. The lost dog _____ up and down the road.
- Ⓐ gathered
- Ⓑ clustered
- Ⓒ cheered
- Ⓓ wandered

5. The team _____ by the coach before the game.
- Ⓐ amazing
- Ⓑ wander
- Ⓒ clustered
- Ⓓ waved

Comprehension

6. Which word tells what Wilson is like at the beginning of the story?

Ⓐ friendly   Ⓑ bossy

Ⓒ happy   Ⓓ shy

7. The story takes place mostly _____.

Ⓐ at home   Ⓑ in the school

Ⓒ in the park   Ⓓ on the bus

8. When the story begins, how does Wilson get home from school?

Ⓐ He walks home.   Ⓑ He calls his mom.

Ⓒ He takes the bus.   Ⓓ He rides his bike.

9. On reading days, everyone but Wilson _____.

Ⓐ reads a story aloud   Ⓑ sits alone

Ⓒ sits in a group   Ⓓ sits with a partner

10. Why doesn't Wilson laugh when the children are playing in the snow?

Ⓐ He hates snow.   Ⓑ He is reading.

Ⓒ He is busy.   Ⓓ He is alone.

11. Why is Sara called a "new girl"?

Ⓐ She always wears new clothes.

Ⓑ She is new in the class.

Ⓒ She is the youngest girl in the class.

Ⓓ She is always making new friends.

12. How are Wilson and Sara alike for one day?

Ⓐ They smile all the time.

Ⓑ They eat lunch together.

Ⓒ They push their desks away from the others.

Ⓓ They do everything alone all day.

13. Why does Sara push her desk into a group of other desks?

Ⓐ She wants to break up the group.

Ⓑ She wants to be part of the group.

Ⓒ Ms. Caraway tells her to join the group.

Ⓓ She wants to be alone.

14. On her second day at school, Sara _____.

Ⓐ plays in the snow

Ⓑ sits with Wilson

Ⓒ reads to the class

Ⓓ sits alone

15. Why does Wilson watch Sara so closely?

Ⓐ He is afraid that she will try to be his friend.

Ⓑ He wants to learn how she makes friends.

Ⓒ He doesn't like her.

Ⓓ He likes the way that she slurps her milk.

Practice Book
Just for You

16. Why does Sara roar a monster roar at Wilson?

 Ⓐ Sara wants to scare Wilson.

 Ⓑ Sara doesn't like Wilson.

 Ⓒ Sara wants him to join in the games.

 Ⓓ The other children tell her to.

17. How is Wilson different after he roars at Sara?

 Ⓐ He has no friends.

 Ⓑ He is scared of Sara.

 Ⓒ Sara is scared of Wilson.

 Ⓓ He isn't alone anymore.

18. Which word best tells what Sara is like?

 Ⓐ friendly   Ⓑ bossy

 Ⓒ silly   Ⓓ shy

19. Why do Wilson's classmates tell Sara not to roar at Wilson?

_____

_____

_____

20. How does Wilson's life change because he roars back at Sara?

_____

_____

_____

Grade 2-1

© Harcourt

Practice Book
Just for You

The Enormous Turnip

Directions: For items 1–18, fill in the circle in front of the correct answer. For items 19–20, write the answer.

Vocabulary

1. The balloon got bigger and bigger until it was _____ .
- Ⓐ enormous
- Ⓑ planted
- Ⓒ turnip
- Ⓓ grew

2. We _____ some flowers in the garden.
- Ⓐ strong
- Ⓑ turnip
- Ⓒ planted
- Ⓓ granddaughter

3. The little seed _____ into a big tree.
- Ⓐ enormous
- Ⓑ grew
- Ⓒ strong
- Ⓓ planted

4. I grew a _____ in my garden.
- Ⓐ turnip
- Ⓑ planted
- Ⓒ strong
- Ⓓ granddaughter

5. This box is a surprise for my _____ .
- Ⓐ enormous
- Ⓑ planted
- Ⓒ granddaughter
- Ⓓ grew

6. The wind was so _____ it blew the tall tree over.
- Ⓐ planted
- Ⓑ turnip
- Ⓒ grew
- Ⓓ strong

© Harcourt

Practice Book
Just for You

Grade 2-1

Comprehension

7. This story takes place _____ .

   (A) last week   (B) last year

   (C) in the future   (D) a long time ago

8. "The Enormous Turnip" is most like a _____ .

   (A) poem   (B) true story

   (C) folktale   (D) play

9. Where does the turnip grow?

   (A) on a bush   (B) in a store

   (C) on a tree   (D) in the ground

10. The old man tells the turnip to grow sweet. In this story, <u>sweet</u> means to _____ .

   (A) look like a lemon   (B) taste good

   (C) taste bitter   (D) feel like a rock

11. The old man also tells the little turnip to grow _____ .

   (A) deep purple outside   (B) golden yellow inside

   (C) very long   (D) strong

12. Who first tries to pull up the turnip?

   (A) the dog   (B) the old woman

   (C) the cat   (D) the old man

13. The old man calls first to the _____ .

Ⓐ old woman   Ⓑ granddaughter

Ⓒ mouse   Ⓓ dog

14. Whom does the granddaughter ask to help?

Ⓐ the mouse   Ⓑ the cat

Ⓒ the dog   Ⓓ the old woman

15. The last to help pull is the _____ .

Ⓐ cat   Ⓑ mouse

Ⓒ granddaughter   Ⓓ dog

16. "The Enormous Turnip" is about _____ .

Ⓐ working on a farm

Ⓑ pulling up a turnip

Ⓒ selling a turnip

Ⓓ a strong mouse

17. What lesson does this story teach?

Ⓐ It is fun to plant vegetables.

Ⓑ The old man could not pull up the turnip by himself.

Ⓒ When everyone helps, a job can get done.

Ⓓ A mouse and a cat can be friends.

© Harcourt

Grade 2-1

18. Why does the writer keep saying some parts again and again?

Ⓐ to make the story fun to tell and to listen to

Ⓑ to show that the turnip is sweet

Ⓒ to make the story longer

Ⓓ to show that turnips are strong

19. Is this story real or make-believe? Tell why.

_____

_____

_____

_____

_____

20. List the people and animals who try to pull up the turnip. Name them in the order that they begin pulling.

_____

_____

_____

_____

_____

© Harcourt

Practice Book
Just for You

Helping Out

Directions: For items 1–18, fill in the circle in front of the correct answer. For items 19–20, write the answer.

Vocabulary

1. I like to do my _____ in the morning.
- Ⓐ chores
- Ⓑ simple
- Ⓒ sprout
- Ⓓ alongside

2. I have a _____ chore for you to do.
- Ⓐ sprout
- Ⓑ planted
- Ⓒ learn
- Ⓓ simple

3. My dad always uses a _____ at his work.
- Ⓐ sprout
- Ⓑ tool
- Ⓒ simple
- Ⓓ dull

4. The car is parked _____ a big bus.
- Ⓐ engine
- Ⓑ sprout
- Ⓒ alongside
- Ⓓ simple

5. Sam worked on the car's _____ all day.
- Ⓐ simple
- Ⓑ sprout
- Ⓒ engine
- Ⓓ enormous

6. The seeds will _____ in a week.
- Ⓐ alongside
- Ⓑ sprout
- Ⓒ simple
- Ⓓ pick

Grade 2-1

Comprehension

7. The author of this book feels that _____.

  Ⓐ most jobs do not need children helping out

  Ⓑ children can help adults in many ways

  Ⓒ adults don't want any help

  Ⓓ children should not hand tools to adults

8. Why did the author write this book?

  Ⓐ to help parents find jobs for their children

  Ⓑ to get his readers to write stories

  Ⓒ to tell how children can help others

  Ⓓ to tell where to get a job that pays

9. The author of this book says one way to help is to _____.

  Ⓐ hand someone a tool

  Ⓑ ride your bike

  Ⓒ eat turnips

  Ⓓ get your hands dirty

10. When does the author say to plant a vegetable garden?

  Ⓐ in the spring   Ⓑ in the summer

  Ⓒ in the autumn   Ⓓ in the winter

11. Why does the author think it is fun to wash a car on a hot summer's day?

  Ⓐ It is sunny.   Ⓑ The car gets clean.

  Ⓒ You can use soap.   Ⓓ You can keep cool.

12. In this book, a dirty job is _____.

  Ⓐ washing a car

  Ⓑ changing the oil in a car

  Ⓒ feeding a baby

  Ⓓ helping a teacher at school

13. This book says one way to help a teacher is to _____.

  Ⓐ pass out papers

  Ⓑ hand out lunch

  Ⓒ pick up the playground

  Ⓓ clean the classroom

14. In this book, which chore is a fun one?

  Ⓐ washing the car   Ⓑ planting seeds

  Ⓒ raking leaves   Ⓓ feeding a baby

15. For the author, how did it feel to work with adults?

  Ⓐ like the worst times in his life

  Ⓑ like being treated as a baby

  Ⓒ like being almost a grown-up

  Ⓓ like doing things that he hated

16. What does the author think is the best thing about helping?

  Ⓐ getting paid

  Ⓑ having fun

  Ⓒ getting closer to someone

  Ⓓ learning a new job

17. The book suggests that if you do a job well, you may _____.

Ⓐ do the job faster

Ⓑ get paid for doing it

Ⓒ get more work

Ⓓ have fun doing the job

18. This book is most like a _____.

Ⓐ folktale   Ⓑ photo essay

Ⓒ play   Ⓓ true story

19. At school, what things can you do to keep your classroom neat and clean?

_____

_____

_____

_____

_____

20. How can you help in a garden?

_____

_____

_____

_____

_____

Mr. Putter and Tabby Fly the Plane

Directions: For items 1–18, fill in the circle in front of the correct answer. For items 19–20, write the answer.

Vocabulary

1. Read the _____ before you begin the test.
- (A) twitch
- (B) worry
- (C) lunches
- (D) directions

2. Will you keep your _____ to me?
- (A) twitch
- (B) promise
- (C) cranes
- (D) worry

3. I will help you, so you don't need to _____ .
- (A) twitch
- (B) cranes
- (C) worry
- (D) will

4. Cats sometimes _____ when they are not happy.
- (A) promise
- (B) twitch
- (C) cranes
- (D) directions

5. The workers use _____ to move the big beams.
- (A) worry
- (B) twitch
- (C) cranes
- (D) promise

© Harcourt

Grade 2-1

Grade 2-1

Comprehension

6. This book is most like a _____ .

   (A) story book   (B) science book

   (C) play   (D) poem

7. Where does this book mostly take place?

   (A) in Mr. Putter's car

   (B) in Mr. Putter's house

   (C) inside the toy store

   (D) outside Mr. Putter's house

8. Why does Mr. Putter think that he should not like toys?

   (A) Tabby does not like the toy store.

   (B) He and Tabby always stop at the toy store.

   (C) Old people should not like toys anymore.

   (D) Tabby is afraid of toys that move.

9. Tabby gets the hiccups from toys that _____ .

   (A) are pop-ups   (B) fly

   (C) beep   (D) are wind-ups

10. What does Mr. Putter like to play with the most?

   (A) pop-ups   (B) dump trucks

   (C) cranes   (D) planes

11. Ace Junkers, biplanes, and monoplanes are all things that _____ .
   Ⓐ walk   Ⓑ fly
   Ⓒ you throw away   Ⓓ float

12. What has Mr. Putter wanted to do all his life?
   Ⓐ fly a real plane   Ⓑ go for a plane ride
   Ⓒ fly a toy plane   Ⓓ work in a toy store

13. How is a biplane different from other planes?
   Ⓐ It has two flags on the tail.
   Ⓑ It has two wings on each side.
   Ⓒ It has two radio controls.
   Ⓓ It is red and white.

14. Why does Mr. Putter buy the toy biplane?
   Ⓐ It has two wings on each side.
   Ⓑ It can fly.
   Ⓒ It is white and red.
   Ⓓ It is a wind-up plane.

15. What does Mr. Putter promise Tabby?
   Ⓐ a plate of tuna
   Ⓑ tea with milk
   Ⓒ tea and an English muffin
   Ⓓ an English muffin

Grade 2-1

Practice Book
Just for You

16. What is the first thing Mr. Putter does when he gets home?

 Ⓐ He feeds Tabby.

 Ⓑ He reads the directions for flying the plane.

 Ⓒ He takes the plane out to the backyard.

 Ⓓ He puts Tabby in the house.

17. How many times does Mr. Putter try to fly the plane without getting it to fly?

 Ⓐ one time   Ⓑ two times

 Ⓒ three times   Ⓓ five times

18. How does Mr. Putter get the little plane to fly?

 Ⓐ He reads the directions over and over.

 Ⓑ He asks the plane to be good.

 Ⓒ He tells the plane that it is the best plane in the world.

 Ⓓ He asks the plane to be brave.

19. Why does Tabby feel sad when the plane will not fly?

_____

_____

20. Name one thing Tabby does to make Mr. Putter feel better.

_____

_____

Hedgehog Bakes a Cake

Directions: For items 1–18, fill in the circle in front of the correct answer. For items 19–20, write the answer.

Vocabulary

1. We _____ butter on the bread.
- (A) perfect
- (B) recipe
- (C) smeared
- (D) barked

2. Dad poured the cake _____ in the pan.
- (A) buttery
- (B) batter
- (C) smeared
- (D) recipe

3. Following a _____ is like following directions.
- (A) yellow cake
- (B) buttery
- (C) perfect
- (D) recipe

4. My hands are _____ from the toast.
- (A) buttery
- (B) batter
- (C) perfect
- (D) recipe

5. We baked a _____ for the party.
- (A) perfect
- (B) yellow cake
- (C) buttery
- (D) recipe

6. It is the _____ day to walk in the woods.
- (A) batter
- (B) smeared
- (C) perfect
- (D) buttery

Practice Book
Just for You

Comprehension

7. This is not a true story because _____ .

Ⓐ animals do not bake cakes

Ⓑ the story took place long ago

Ⓒ it is too long

Ⓓ the characters are real people

8. This book mostly takes place in _____ .

Ⓐ Hedgehog's kitchen   Ⓑ Rabbit's yard

Ⓒ Owl's nest   Ⓓ Squirrel's house

9. Which character is this story mostly about?

Ⓐ Owl   Ⓑ Rabbit

Ⓒ Hedgehog   Ⓓ Squirrel

10. How does Rabbit make a cake?

Ⓐ He follows a recipe.

Ⓑ He measures some things.

Ⓒ He guesses how much of each thing to put in a cake.

Ⓓ He measures everything carefully.

11. Why does Rabbit say someone is calling him?

Ⓐ Rabbit doesn't want to mix the cake anymore.

Ⓑ Squirrel is at the door.

Ⓒ Rabbit hears his mother yelling his name.

Ⓓ Owl is hooting for him to come outside.

Practice Book
Just for You

12. Why does Hedgehog want to turn down Owl's help?

     Ⓐ The cake is ready to put in the oven.

     Ⓑ Rabbit and Squirrel have not been any help.

     Ⓒ Hedgehog does not want to share the cake with Owl.

     Ⓓ Owl wants to make a white cake.

13. Why does Hedgehog let Owl help?

     Ⓐ Owl knows how hot the oven should be.

     Ⓑ Squirrel asks Owl to help.

     Ⓒ Hedgehog does not want Owl to feel left out.

     Ⓓ Owl says she will follow the recipe.

14. What does Squirrel think will happen after the cake is baked?

     Ⓐ Hedgehog will put frosting on the cake.

     Ⓑ Hedgehog will share the cake with his friends.

     Ⓒ All the friends will help clean up the kitchen.

     Ⓓ It will be time for breakfast.

15. Hedgehog makes a second cake. What is the only thing he uses from the first cake?

     Ⓐ the eggs Squirrel cracked

     Ⓑ the batter Rabbit mixed

     Ⓒ a friend's secret recipe

     Ⓓ the pan Owl buttered

Grade 2-1

© Harcourt

Practice Book
Just for You

Grade 2-1

16. How do Hedgehog's friends know when the cake is done?
Ⓐ They smell it.
Ⓑ They see it through a window.
Ⓒ They are cleaned up.
Ⓓ They look in the oven.

17. How many slices of cake does each friend eat?
Ⓐ none　　　　Ⓑ one slice
Ⓒ two slices　　Ⓓ three slices

18. What does Hedgehog say to his friends so they will not help him bake another time?
Ⓐ "I'll try to bake the next cake by myself."
Ⓑ "You don't know how to bake a cake."
Ⓒ "I don't want you in my kitchen."
Ⓓ "I don't need your help."

19. Why does Hedgehog lock his kitchen door?

_____

_____

20. Rabbit and Hedgehog have different ways of making a cake. Explain how Hedgehog makes a cake.

_____

_____

© Harcourt

Lemonade for Sale

Directions: For items 1–18, fill in the circle in front of the correct answer. For items 19–20, write the answer.

Vocabulary

1. There are four _____ in our club.
Ⓐ arrived   Ⓑ glum
Ⓒ members   Ⓓ winters

2. The two boxes _____ at the same time.
Ⓐ rebuild   Ⓑ arrived
Ⓒ announced   Ⓓ members

3. Pat _____ that the game will start soon.
Ⓐ members   Ⓑ arrived
Ⓒ glum   Ⓓ announced

4. Sam has been _____ all day because it is raining and cold.
Ⓐ rebuild   Ⓑ arrived
Ⓒ announced   Ⓓ glum

5. We had to _____ the playhouse because the wind blew it down.
Ⓐ announced   Ⓑ rebuild
Ⓒ members   Ⓓ arrived

Practice Book
Just for You

Comprehension

6. This book is most like a _____ .

  Ⓐ play   Ⓑ story book

  Ⓒ cookbook   Ⓓ poem

7. In this story, what do they use to make lemonade?

  Ⓐ lemons, oranges, sugar

  Ⓑ water, lemons, cups

  Ⓒ lemons, sugar, ice

  Ⓓ oranges, sugar, ice

8. Who squeezes the lemons?

  Ⓐ Matthew   Ⓑ Petey

  Ⓒ Meg   Ⓓ Danny

9. What problem does the Elm Street Kids' Club have?

  Ⓐ Some kids do not want to belong anymore.

  Ⓑ The kids need money to rebuild their clubhouse.

  Ⓒ The club needs new members.

  Ⓓ The kids want a bigger clubhouse.

10. Where does this story take place?

  Ⓐ inside a mall   Ⓑ in the country

  Ⓒ on Elm Street   Ⓓ at a grocery store

Practice Book
Just for You

11. How many cups of lemonade do they need to sell?
- Ⓐ about 20 cups a day for a week
- Ⓑ 30 to 40 cups a day for a week
- Ⓒ 30 to 40 cups a day for a month
- Ⓓ 56 cups a day for a month

12. What does Sheri offer to do?
- Ⓐ make a bar graph
- Ⓑ draw a sign of a pitcher of lemonade
- Ⓒ count people who walk by
- Ⓓ count the lemons that they use

13. "Not bad. Not bad," chattered Petey. In this story, chattered means _____ .
- Ⓐ laughed
- Ⓑ sang
- Ⓒ asked
- Ⓓ squawked

14. Why is Sheri's method of keeping track of sales a good one?
- Ⓐ She lists the days of the week along the bottom.
- Ⓑ She lists the number of cups up the side.
- Ⓒ The kids can see how many cups they sell each day.
- Ⓓ The kids can see how many lemons they use each day.

Practice Book
Just for You

15. Why are lemonade sales poor on Thursday?

   Ⓐ It rains.

   Ⓑ The Elm Street Kids' Club runs out of lemons.

   Ⓒ There is a hot dog stand on the corner.

   Ⓓ There is a juggler on the corner.

16. Sheri whispers to Jed. What does she ask him?

   Ⓐ if he has juggled for a long time

   Ⓑ if he will juggle next to the lemonade stand

   Ⓒ if he likes lemonade

   Ⓓ if he likes Petey

17. Which word best describes Jed?

   Ⓐ friendly   Ⓑ foolish

   Ⓒ angry   Ⓓ selfish

18. On which day does the Elm Street Kids' Club sell the most lemonade?

   Ⓐ on Monday   Ⓑ on Tuesday

   Ⓒ on Wednesday   Ⓓ on Friday

19. Who says everything two times?

_____

_____

20. What is the weather like in the story?

_____

_____

Johnny Appleseed

Directions: For items 1–18, fill in the circle in front of the correct answer. For items 19–20, write the answer.

Vocabulary

1. There are apple _____ near our house.
- (A) frontier
- (B) survive
- (C) orchards
- (D) mornings

2. Can you _____ a lion?
- (A) tame
- (B) nearby
- (C) wild
- (D) twitch

3. They moved west to the _____ lands.
- (A) survive
- (B) frontier
- (C) tame
- (D) autumn

4. Many _____ animals live in the woods.
- (A) survive
- (B) frontier
- (C) orchards
- (D) wild

5. We can walk to the park because it is _____ .
- (A) tame
- (B) survive
- (C) nearby
- (D) sometimes

6. On the frontier, it was sometimes hard to _____ .
- (A) tame
- (B) orchards
- (C) survive
- (D) nearby

Practice Book
Just for You

Comprehension

7. This book is most like a _____ .

Ⓒ tall tale   Ⓓ play

Ⓔ poem   Ⓕ letter

8. In this book the narrator _____ .

Ⓒ wears a stewpot on his head

Ⓓ is who the book is about

Ⓔ fills in the details

Ⓕ does not like Johnny

9. How many half-brothers and half-sisters does Johnny Appleseed have?

Ⓒ seven half-brothers and half-sisters

Ⓓ nine half-brothers and half-sisters

Ⓔ ten half-brothers and half-sisters

Ⓕ eleven half-brothers and half-sisters

10. When does the play take place?

Ⓒ a few years ago   Ⓓ a long time ago

Ⓔ last year   Ⓕ last month

11. Johnny Appleseed's real name is _____ .

Ⓒ John Apple   Ⓓ John Tree Planter

Ⓔ John Chapman   Ⓕ John Seeds

Grade 2-1

© Harcourt

Practice Book
Just for You

12. In Scene One, Johnny's neighbors are moving _____ .
Ⓐ somewhere out west
Ⓑ to Pennsylvania
Ⓒ to Massachusetts
Ⓓ back to their hometown

13. Settlers can't take their apple trees to the west. So what does Johnny do?
Ⓐ gives settlers sacks of seeds to take with them
Ⓑ goes west and plants apple seeds
Ⓒ travels to the west and gives out seeds
Ⓓ sells apples in the west

14. How do the frontier children feel when they first see Johnny?
Ⓐ They are proud to meet someone so famous.
Ⓑ They are curious.
Ⓒ They are thankful for his hard work.
Ⓓ They are afraid because he looks strange.

15. Johnny often says, "I've got itchy feet." What does he mean?
Ⓐ He always wants to go see new places.
Ⓑ He needs new shoes.
Ⓒ He has a rash on his feet.
Ⓓ He has insect bites on his feet.

Grade 2-1

Practice Book
Just for You

Grade 2-1

16. How do Young Wolf and Ten Horses feel about Johnny?

Ⓐ They think that Johnny is bad.

Ⓑ They warn Johnny about the she-bear.

Ⓒ They like Johnny and know he tells the truth.

Ⓓ They think that Johnny is lazy.

17. How many years does Johnny travel and plant trees?

Ⓐ 7 years   Ⓑ 23 years

Ⓒ 48 years   Ⓓ 71 years

18. How are Pennsylvania, Ohio, and Indiana different because of Johnny?

Ⓐ Bears live there.

Ⓑ There are many apple orchards.

Ⓒ Many people come from the east to live there.

Ⓓ These places have many towns and schools.

19. Johnny has two nicknames—Johnny Appleseed and Tree Planter. Why did people give him these names?

_____

_____

20. Name two foods that you can make with apples.

_____

_____

From Seed to Plant

Directions: For items 1–18, fill in the circle in front of the correct answer. For items 19–20, write the answer.

Vocabulary

1. You can eat the apple when it _____ .
   Ⓐ protects   Ⓑ ripens
   Ⓒ streams   Ⓓ nutrition

2. Your flowers are _____ .
   Ⓐ nutrition   Ⓑ protects
   Ⓒ between   Ⓓ beautiful

3. We saw fish in the _____ .
   Ⓐ beautiful   Ⓑ streams
   Ⓒ nutrition   Ⓓ protects

4. We need to eat many foods to have good _____ .
   Ⓐ protects   Ⓑ beautiful
   Ⓒ nutrition   Ⓓ ripens

5. Some animals have a fur coat that _____ them from the cold.
   Ⓐ protects   Ⓑ ripens
   Ⓒ beautiful   Ⓓ streams

© Harcourt

Grade 2-1

Practice Book
Just for You

Grade 2-1

Comprehension

6. The beginning of a new plant is inside a _____ .

Ⓐ flower   Ⓑ petal

Ⓒ shoot   Ⓓ seed

7. Which is true about all seeds?

Ⓐ Seeds grow into the kind of plant they came from.

Ⓑ All seeds have the same shape.

Ⓒ All seeds look the same.

Ⓓ All seeds are the same color.

8. Flowers have parts called stamens. Stamens make _____ .

Ⓐ fruit   Ⓑ berries

Ⓒ nectar   Ⓓ pollen

9. After flowers are pollinated, they _____ .

Ⓐ make nectar

Ⓑ begin to make seeds

Ⓒ become sweet tasting

Ⓓ begin to bloom

10. When are seeds ready to become new plants?

Ⓐ before the fruit or pods get ripe

Ⓑ after the fruit or pods get ripe

Ⓒ before the flower is pollinated

Ⓓ after the flower is pollinate

Practice Book
Just for You

11. Pollen moves from flower to flower. Seeds scatter in many directions. What can make both these things happen?

Ⓐ wind   Ⓑ water

Ⓒ nectar   Ⓓ squirrels

12. Having hooks that stick to fur, floating on water, and being buried by animals are all ways that _____ .

Ⓐ plants protect themselves

Ⓑ seeds get to different places

Ⓒ flowers get pollen

Ⓓ sprouts grow

13. How are a seed coat and the fruit or pod around a seed alike?

Ⓐ They make seeds pretty.

Ⓑ They protect seeds.

Ⓒ They make seeds open up.

Ⓓ They make seeds full of poison.

14. What three things does a seed need to start growing?

Ⓐ soil, water, nectar   Ⓑ soil, pollen, sun

Ⓒ water, salt, sun   Ⓓ soil, water, sun

Grade 2-1

Practice Book
Just for You

15. Why does a seed need roots?

   Ⓐ to get sunlight

   Ⓑ to germinate

   Ⓒ to get water and minerals

   Ⓓ to get air

16. When the seed begins to grow, it is called _____ .

   Ⓐ pollination   Ⓑ direction

   Ⓒ germination   Ⓓ nutrition

17. People eat some seeds, fruits, and pods because _____ .

   Ⓐ they are full of nutrition

   Ⓑ the plants have pretty flowers

   Ⓒ they grow in the ground

   Ⓓ the roots take in water

18. This book is _____ .

   Ⓐ a play   Ⓑ fiction

   Ⓒ a tall tale   Ⓓ nonfiction

19. How do insects move pollen from flower to flower?

_____

_____

20. Why did the author write this book?

_____

_____

The Secret Life of Trees

Directions: For items 1–18, fill in the circle in front of the correct answer. For items 19–20, write the answer.

Vocabulary

1. When did they _____ the surprise?
Ⓐ discover   Ⓑ shed
Ⓒ source   Ⓓ south

2. We need _____ to run the long race.
Ⓐ source   Ⓑ forecast
Ⓒ energy   Ⓓ discover

3. Some trees _____ their leaves in autumn.
Ⓐ discover   Ⓑ source
Ⓒ forecast   Ⓓ shed

4. The sun is a good _____ of light.
Ⓐ source   Ⓑ forecast
Ⓒ energy   Ⓓ discover

5. There is a _____ of rain today.
Ⓐ discover   Ⓑ forecast
Ⓒ shed   Ⓓ tallest

Comprehension

6. This book is most like a _____ .
Ⓐ nonfiction book Ⓑ math book
Ⓒ story book   Ⓓ play

Grade 2-1

Practice Book
Just for You

7. "The Secret Life of Trees" is a good title for this book because it tells about _____ .

Ⓐ trees that live in the tropics

Ⓑ trees and the animals that live in them

Ⓒ how long it takes a tree to grow

Ⓓ the many things that are made from trees

8. This book says _____ is the heaviest thing on Earth.

Ⓐ an elephant   Ⓑ a chestnut

Ⓒ a tree   Ⓓ wood

9. The tree's bark protects the _____ .

Ⓐ leaves and branches

Ⓑ trunk and branches

Ⓒ roots and trunk

Ⓓ roots and leaves

10. A tree gets its food from the _____ .

Ⓐ cones   Ⓑ bark

Ⓒ birds   Ⓓ leaves

11. A tree can live _____ .

Ⓐ without sun and water

Ⓑ in a hard shell

Ⓒ longer than other living things

Ⓓ without water and soil

© Harcourt

Practice Book
Just for You

12. Which trees lose their leaves in winter?

   Ⓐ conifers   Ⓑ broad-leaved trees

   Ⓒ pine trees   Ⓓ coconut palms

13. Seeds may never grow into a tree because _____ .

   Ⓐ pine cones are seeds

   Ⓑ seeds have hard shells

   Ⓒ trees drop seeds to the ground

   Ⓓ animals may eat the seeds

14. The sugar pine cone is _____ long.

   Ⓐ half an inch   Ⓑ two inches

   Ⓒ two feet   Ⓓ ten feet

15. Pine cones forecast a storm by _____ .

   Ⓐ opening their scales

   Ⓑ dropping to the ground

   Ⓒ turning brown

   Ⓓ closing their scales

16. The tallest tree alive today is growing in _____ .

   Ⓐ a wet jungle   Ⓑ California

   Ⓒ Texas   Ⓓ a tropical country

17. Which two things are made from wood?

   Ⓐ bikes and tables   Ⓑ pens and paper

   Ⓒ books and paper   Ⓓ insects and bugs

Grade 2-1

Practice Book
Just for You

18. The branches of conifers are bouncy so they
will _____ .

Ⓐ break when covered with snow

Ⓑ lose their leaves in winter

Ⓒ not snap when covered with snow

Ⓓ change color in the fall

19. Why can a palm tree's seed grow without water?

_____

_____

_____

_____

_____

20. What does the author mean by "in summer a tree is
an animal hotel"?

_____

_____

_____

_____

_____

© Harcourt

Watermelon Day

Directions: For items 1–18, fill in the circle in front of the correct answer. For items 19–20, write the answer.

Vocabulary

1. The baby bird hid _____ its mother's wings.
Ⓐ beneath   Ⓑ wrinkled
Ⓒ knelt   Ⓓ end

2. The waters of the lake _____ in the sun.
Ⓐ wrinkled   Ⓑ shimmered
Ⓒ knelt   Ⓓ relay race

3. She was safe and _____ in her bed.
Ⓐ snug   Ⓑ wrinkled
Ⓒ beneath   Ⓓ front

4. We _____ in the dirt to weed the garden.
Ⓐ wrinkled   Ⓑ knelt
Ⓒ beneath   Ⓓ snug

5. Will you iron the _____ dress?
Ⓐ shimmered   Ⓑ beneath
Ⓒ wrinkled   Ⓓ knelt

6. In the _____, each member of the team ran very fast.
Ⓐ relay race   Ⓑ beneath
Ⓒ shimmered   Ⓓ wrinkled

Grade 2-1

Comprehension

7. This book is most like a true story because _____ .

Ⓐ the people could be real

Ⓑ the place could not be real

Ⓒ the book is full of jokes

Ⓓ it is a play

8. When Jesse first finds her watermelon, how big is it?

Ⓐ a little smaller than the other watermelons

Ⓑ as big as Jesse's fist

Ⓒ bigger than the other watermelons

Ⓓ as big as its mama's fuzzy leaf

9. Pappy says that Jesse's watermelon will be "just right for a Watermelon Day." What does he mean?

Ⓐ All the relatives will come for food and fun.

Ⓑ The watermelon is the biggest in town.

Ⓒ The watermelon might win a prize.

Ⓓ Uncle Ike will come for a visit.

10. Jesse finds her watermelon in the _____ .

Ⓐ early spring   Ⓑ autumn

Ⓒ late summer   Ⓓ early summer

11. At first, the watermelon makes a dull sound like _____ .

Ⓐ a knock on the door   Ⓑ Pappy's boots

Ⓒ someone whistling   Ⓓ someone walking

12. In this story, what does the author mean by "a dark green rind"?

Ⓐ the inside of a watermelon

Ⓑ a watermelon patch

Ⓒ the skin of the watermelon

Ⓓ the sweetest song

13. How hot does the weather get that summer?

Ⓐ There is always a blue sky.

Ⓑ It is never too hot or too cold.

Ⓒ Bare feet burn in the sand.

Ⓓ Everyone has to wear sweaters.

14. Watermelons grow well _____ .

Ⓐ near cool lakes   Ⓑ in sandy soil

Ⓒ on rocky soil   Ⓓ in shady spots

15. Why does Pappy put the watermelon in the lake "beneath the deep blue shade" of the willow tree?

Ⓐ The shaded water is colder.

Ⓑ The branches hide the watermelon.

Ⓒ That part of the lake is nearest to the house.

Ⓓ Branches keep the watermelon from floating away.

16. On Watermelon Day, what is one thing that happens while the watermelon floats?

Ⓐ The watermelon opens. Ⓑ Jesse sings.

Ⓒ Pappy swings.   Ⓓ People play softball.

© Harcourt

Grade 2-1

Practice Book
Just for You

17. The watermelon was cold enough to eat when "the sun began to sink." What time of day was that?

Ⓐ evening   Ⓑ noon

Ⓒ night   Ⓓ morning

18. In the story, <u>Craaack</u>!!!, <u>Splittt</u>!!!, and <u>Poppp</u>!!! are sounds made by _____ .

Ⓐ Pappy's boots hitting the floor

Ⓑ the game of freeze tag

Ⓒ the watermelon being opened

Ⓓ the watermelon landing in the lake

19. Jesse feels that "the day stretched like a lazy ol' cat." What does she mean?

_____

_____

_____

20. During Watermelon Day, what does Jesse keep asking Pappy?

_____

_____

_____

© Harcourt

Practice Book
Just for You

Pumpkin Fiesta

Directions: For items 1–18, fill in the circle in front of the correct answer. For items 19–20, write the answer.

Vocabulary

1. The _____ are covered with flowers.
  Ⓐ vines   Ⓑ village
  Ⓒ crown   Ⓓ boasted

2. We have a big fiesta each year in my _____ .
  Ⓐ crown   Ⓑ boasted
  Ⓒ vines   Ⓓ village

3. The king has a sparkling _____ on his head.
  Ⓐ crept   Ⓑ village
  Ⓒ crown   Ⓓ boasted

4. We _____ down the path so no one would see us.
  Ⓐ boasted   Ⓑ crept
  Ⓒ crown   Ⓓ vines

5. "I made a fine yellow cake!" she _____ .
  Ⓐ boasted   Ⓑ crown
  Ⓒ crept   Ⓓ village

Comprehension

6. In this book a <u>fiesta</u> is a _____ .
  Ⓐ fair   Ⓑ play
  Ⓒ party   Ⓓ dance

Practice Book
Just for You

7. What problem does Foolish Fernando have?

Ⓐ He does not like his village.

Ⓑ He wants to win the pumpkin crown.

Ⓒ He wants to move to Old Juana's village.

Ⓓ His bull is sick.

8. Fernando is not proud of Old Juana because _____ .

Ⓐ she is old

Ⓑ she grows the best pumpkins

Ⓒ he wants her burro

Ⓓ he wants her plot of land

9. Why does Fernando put on a dress and straw hat?

Ⓐ He thinks they will help him to grow the best pumpkins.

Ⓑ The straw hat will protect him from the sun.

Ⓒ Toro told him to.

Ⓓ Old Juana likes faded dresses.

10. Juana plants her seeds very carefully.
Fernando _____ .

Ⓐ plants his carefully   Ⓑ scatters his seeds

Ⓒ loses his seeds   Ⓓ does not hoe

11. How are Juana's vines different from Fernando's?

Ⓐ Juana's vines are scrawny.

Ⓑ Juana's vines have bugs on them.

Ⓒ Juana's vines are big and strong.

Ⓓ Juana has no vines.

© Harcourt

Practice Book
Just for You

12. Gorda, Linda, and Blush Bottom are the names of _____ .

Ⓐ Fernando's bulls

Ⓑ Juana's burros

Ⓒ Juana's pumpkins

Ⓓ Fernando's pumpkins

13. Why does Toro run away from Fernando?

Ⓐ Toro wants to play.

Ⓑ Toro likes the corner of the field.

Ⓒ Toro likes to eat bugs.

Ⓓ Toro is embarrassed by Fernando.

14. On the night before the fiesta, Fernando _____ .

Ⓐ went to bed late

Ⓑ cut Juana's pumpkins

Ⓒ stole Juana's burro

Ⓓ chased Toro in the field

15. Why does Old Juana cut her pumpkin vines after the pumpkins are gone?

Ⓐ She wants to give them to Fernando.

Ⓑ Ducita will eat them.

Ⓒ They will prove someone stole her pumpkins.

Ⓓ The mayor likes pumpkin vines.

Grade 2-1

16. The crowd chants "¡Viva Juana!" because they are _____ .
  Ⓐ mad at Juana   Ⓑ proud of her
  Ⓒ sorry for her   Ⓓ calling for her

17. In the end, you can tell Old Juana is not mad at Foolish Fernando because she _____ .
  Ⓐ gives Gorda to him
  Ⓑ promises to teach him how to grow pumpkins
  Ⓒ lets him have the pumpkin crown
  Ⓓ sings with the mayor and Foolish Fernando

18. This book is most like _____ .
  Ⓐ nonfiction   Ⓑ a tall tale
  Ⓒ a folktale   Ⓓ a play

19. How can you tell that Foolish Fernando is sorry he stole the pumpkins?

_____

_____

_____

20. What secret will Old Juana teach to Foolish Fernando?

_____

_____

_____

Practice Book
Just for You